LADIES of the FIELD

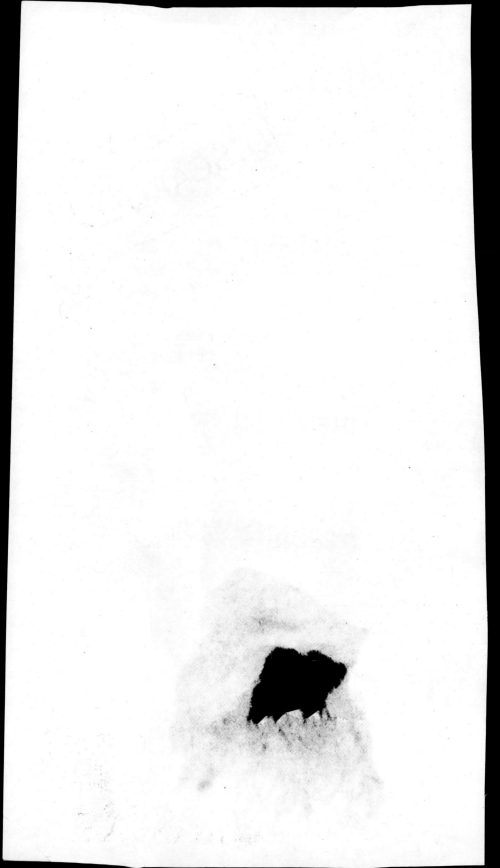

AMANDA ADAMS

LADIES of the FIELD

· · · · · · EARLY · · · · · ·

WOMEN ARCHAEOLOGISTS

AND THEIR SEARCH FOR ADVENTURE

GREYSTONE BOOKS

D&M PUBLISHERS INC.

Vancouver / Toronto / Berkeley

Greystone Books
An imprint of D&M Publishers Inc.
2323 Quebec Street, Suite 201
Vancouver BC Canada V5T 4S7
www.greystonebooks.com

Cataloguing in Publication data available from Library and Archives Canada
ISBN: 978-1-55365-433-9 (pbk.)
ISBN: 978-1-55365-641-8 (ebook)

Editing by Nancy Flight
Copyediting by Lara Kordic
Cover and text design by Heather Pringle
Front cover photographs:
(top left) © Hulton-Deutsch Collection/CORBIS;
(top right) © Smith College Archives, Smith College;
(bottom right) © Harry Todd/Getty Images
Front cover background image:
The Map House of London/Stockbyte/Getty Images
Printed and bound in Canada by Friesens
Printed on acid-free, 100% post-consumer paper
Distributed in the U.S. by Publishers Group West

We gratefully acknowledge the financial support of
the Canada Council for the Arts, the British Columbia Arts Council,
the Province of British Columbia through the Book Publishing Tax Credit,
and the Government of Canada through the Canada Book Fund
for our publishing activities.

Mixed Sources
Cert no. SW-COC-001271
© 1996 FSC
FSC

For the two great women in my life:
My mother, Kathy
And in memory of my grandmother Lorraine Shea

CONTENTS

INTRODUCTION

* * * * *

FIELD NOTES

The first women archaeologists were Victorian era adventurers who felt most at home when farthest from it. Canvas tents were their domains, hot Middle Eastern deserts their gardens of inquiry and labor. Thanks to them, conventional ideas about feminine nature—soft, nurturing, submissive—were up-ended. The excavation shovel churned things up, flipped things over, and loosened the stays of gender a little. *Ladies of the Field* tells the stories of seven remarkable women, each a pioneering archaeologist, each a force of nature who possessed intellect and guts. All were convention-breaking and courageous women who burst into the halls of what was then a very young science.

For centuries, archaeology had been little more than a game of treasure hunting, a kind of cowboy science in which men traveled far and wide in search of gold and other trophies to bring home. Early archaeological exploration wasn't much different from looting; it was the khaki-clad branch of art history that emphasized digging and acquiring (nay, stealing) the art. Yet by the mid-nineteenth century, archaeology was shaking off its antiquarian robes. Women were beginning to enter the field, sending a bright signal not just that times had begun to change but that archaeology would too. The nineteenth century was a time when more and more women began rejecting common submission to the patriarchy. It was a time of increasing social turmoil: John Stuart Mill's book *The Subjection of Women* (1869) was causing a stir in its demand for equality between the sexes. Working-class girls were receiving more education than ever before, and even inventions like the typewriter and the telephone eventually helped to bring women out of the house and into the workforce, where their talents could be at least moderately appreciated. Some women were becoming more vocal about their rights and their wants. For most this meant pursuing the right to vote in their home country or the opportunity to simply further their education. For others, it meant climbing mountains, becoming doctors or architects, and fighting for entry into scientific fields. For early women archaeologists, it was by their work—some of it sensuous travelogue, more of it formidable scholarship—that they helped to reshape how we study the past.

The belief persists that women are not mentioned in the early annals of archaeology's history because they weren't there. Not true. Women were present in the archaeological field by the mid- to late 1800s, but they were very few and were often given diminished scholarly treatment by male colleagues. As one scholar explains, "Over the course of the last 150 years, a rigid power structure has been established in archeology. Although men have controlled this power structure throughout the history of the discipline, women have always made significant, if devalued, contributions to archeology."[1] Those neglected contributions are emerging from the shadows today.

Before the 1920s and 30s, when archaeology became more firmly established and its doors were opened to women much more so than ever before, a handful of intrepid ladies chased their love of hidden history. Some worked part-time in museums; others had the financial means to contribute to digs and explorations. But an extraordinary few packed their bags, left the floral sitting rooms and pretty petticoats behind, and embarked on rigorous journeys that took them around the world in pursuit of archaeological wonders. This book is about them.

The pioneering female archaeologists were a diverse group: reckless to some, the smartest and most laudable ladies to others. The very first to "scale the heights" of a camel and touch patent leather shoe to Egyptian sand was Amelia Edwards. Eventually nicknamed the "Godmother of Egyptology," Edwards sailed the Nile on a houseboat as early as 1873, sketching the pyramids and eventually making an archaeological discovery all her own.

Soon after, Jane Dieulafoy burst onto the scene with her archaeologist husband, Marcel. The two of them traveled thousands of miles on pounding horseback through what is now Iran. They set their sights on the ruins of Susa, and Dieulafoy became one of the most celebrated women in Europe, not just because of her archaeological prowess, but because she was a French lady who preferred to wear men's clothing. She even requested and obtained an official permit from the government authorities to do so.

The strong-minded Zelia Nuttall was born in San Francisco and schooled in Europe and eventually made her permanent home in Mexico City, where she became a prominent scholar in Mexican archaeology, a cultural icon in black lace shawl, and master gardener of ancient seeds. She played host to celebrities such as D.H. Lawrence and was a firm believer in modern scientific methods. Nuttall was also famous for finding ancient papers and objects the rest of the world had presumed lost.

Gertrude Bell deserves her own book, and luckily several have been written about her. A legendary lady, she was an insatiable traveler, brilliant intellectual, photographer, diplomat, strategist, and all-around "Queen of the Desert." In Bell's heyday, she was *the* most powerful woman in the British Empire. Her life soars with supreme adventure, and no matter where she was, she always wished "to gaze upon the ruins." The pursuit of archaeology is what structured Bell's expansive wanderings.

In her mid-twenties Harriet Boyd decided she could learn far more about ancient Greece by living there—under its blue sky and white colonnades—than by studying its history in the pages of a library book. By 1900, she was crossing the wine-dark sea to begin ground-breaking excavations at the site of Gournia on the island of Crete. Before leaving Athens she had also developed a reputation as a girl bicycle rider. Newspapers chronicled her daily exploits (even if she was just doing errands); she shocked passersby by touring through Athenian streets in a long dress on a bike with a basket.

Not long after, the world's future best-selling novelist Agatha Christie was sitting at her rickety desk in a humble London flat typing out the draft of one of her first detective stories, *The Mysterious Affair at Styles*. Little did Christie know that she would soon be divorced, onboard the Orient Express alone, happier than she'd ever been, and en route to meet her second husband, Max Mallowan. Together they would spend thirty years inside the trenches of archaeological fieldwork.

Last, there is the enigmatic Dorothy Garrod, a ferociously good scholar who methodically tore down what final barriers still stood that prevented women from joining the ranks of archaeology. Garrod's quest was to discover the very origins of who we are and where we come from. Having lost three brothers to World War I, she dedicated herself to proving her own life worthy not just of one man's accomplishments but rather of three.

All seven women were headstrong, smart, and brave. They had a taste for adventure, a kind of adventure that no longer exists today. In the late nineteenth and early twentieth century, massive swaths of desert remained unmapped, communication moved no faster than a horse's gallop (at least in those deserts where they roamed; the first transatlantic telegraph wasn't sent until the mid-1860s), and to travel at all as a woman—especially as a woman alone—elicited most people's disapproval. Yet here were these seven women who risked everything just so they could dig in the dirt. This book sets out to discover who these extraordinary women were, what made them tick, and why they chose archaeology—a career grounded in mud, bugs, leaky tents, and toil—as their life's consuming passion.

THE VICTORIAN ERA (1837–1901) PROVIDES THE backdrop for all seven women: each was born in or worked during that time. To be a woman archaeologist today requires some sure navigation through a boy's club, but back then, the boy's club was bolted shut. In Victorian times, opportunities for women outside the home were no larger than the tiny embroidery stitches the girls worked on each day. Women could and often needed to work to help support their families, but that labor typically consisted of sewing, washing, domestic service, shoemaking, and factory jobs. The upper echelons of intellectual careers and politics were largely off-limits.

Queen Victoria was in reign, and it is ironic that one of history's most debilitating times for women, socially speaking, was when a queen ruled the Empire.[2] Victorian influence on the private and public spheres of life was felt not only in England but also in France and across the Atlantic in North America. Industrialization was dramatically transforming society: the divide between rich and poor widened, and suddenly, the home and the workplace became two very different and separate spheres. Women were shooed into a domestic role, expected to become chaste "angels of the house," cheerfully on hand to meet the needs of their husbands and children (think of a full-time domestic goddess without an exit strategy or a cocktail hour) while men engaged in the world and its affairs. Rousseau's view on the expectations and education for a woman sum it up:

> All the education of women should bear a relation to men—
> to please, to be useful to them—to possess their love and
> esteem, to educate them in childhood, to nurse them when
> grown up—to counsel, to console, to make their lives pleas-
> ant and sweet; such are the duties of women and should be
> taught to them from infancy.[3]

His eighteenth-century views continued to inform the next century and were frequently cited as the way to go. Females were creatures of service. Their minds should never be taxed because their brainpower was delicate and feeble. Girls were praised for their passivity and obedience, and throughout Queen Victoria's reign (and to some extent after) women's lives were made highly interior, almost invisible, while men assumed a greater public persona and place in the work force. It was a polarizing time of public versus private, male roles versus female roles.

Science didn't help. Scholars gave credence to theories that women were "weak in brain and body." They needed a man's protection from the world. Doctors proclaimed that "love of home, of children, and of domestic duties are the only passions they [women] feel,"[4] that "a reasonable woman should always be contented with what her husband is able to do and should never demand more,"[5] and perhaps most damning, that "any strain upon a girl's intellect is to be dreaded, and any attempt to bring women into competition with men can scarcely escape failure."[6] How the first women archaeologists defied the times! With dirt under their fingernails, living in tents, managing large crews of male workmen, attending universities, smoking men's pipes, wearing trousers, some never married, some never mothers—all were deliciously defiant of the social roles pressed upon them.

These seven foremothers of "inappropriate" behavior blazed a trail that helped other women enter the world and the work of science, but these pioneers also reached even further. Newspaper articles and monthly magazines carried stories of their adventures and accomplishments. Public speaking tours brought thousands to hear them. Slowly, but most surely, they reconfigured the public impression of a woman's worth and dismantled the building blocks of unchecked chauvinism. It was through the seemingly "masculine" work of archaeology—the physical labor, discomforts of the field, the dirt and discovery—that these women helped to revolutionize the very nature of womanhood, or, perhaps more accurately, our understanding of woman's nature. Although actions to address gender inequality had already been stirred in the mid-nineteenth century—rumblings of Britain's women's suffrage movement began in 1866—it was the first women archaeologists who chipped away at the foundations and rationalizations of Victorian age thinking with real tools: steel shovels and excavation picks.

Each woman described here made a significant contribution to archaeology when it was just a fledgling science, but they also illuminate the myriad facets of a woman's world. Some sought adventure and made the world feel bigger; others were drawn to mystery. One worked within a life-long partnership, and another in pure solitude with stingingly clear fast winds at her back. In a letter home to her father, Gertude Bell once exclaimed while traveling alone on horseback through the desert, "How big the world is, how big and how wonderful."[7] The world is big and wonderful, and these women embody the very best of its possibility.

Each chapter tells one woman's story and explores why she chose archaeology as her life's purpose. Did these women find a much bigger and perhaps more wonderful world in the fields of archaeology than they could ever have at home? Did they forsake romantic love for this world? Did they live with any regret? Were these seven women happy in their chosen career, one that afforded them terrific adventures but always required a relentless uphill climb, both literally and metaphorically? And as any archaeologist would want to know, what exactly did these unique women find along the way?

Seven women; surely there must have been more. Many woman worked along the margins of archaeology during the Victorian era and for the next decade or two afterwards. Some of these women, like Sophia Schliemann and Hilda Petrie, were the wives of famous archaeologists. They worked alongside their husbands in the field and no doubt knew their stuff, but the record they left behind is as faint as old carvings on weathered stone. They never published on their own (or not much), and their labor in the field lacked real ownership or autonomy. For

ABOVE: Sophie Schliemann, wife of archaeologist Heinrich Schliemann, wearing the jewels of Helen of Troy, 1876

better or worse, as those wedding vows pronounced, they were wives to their men, and those men authored the reports, led the teams, and took full credit for any discoveries of note. Wives in the field were viewed as extremely useful assistants. They could draw artifacts, keep the lab in order, inventory artifacts, and nurse the wounded field crew, but true scientists they were not. At least not as recorded.

Archaeology thus has several ghosts. For many of the first women who worked in the field, there was no afterlife—no legacy. Their work wasn't registered in the pages of history. The earliest contributions of women in the field are in the style of the man behind the man, or more aptly put, the woman behind her husband, the mere whisper in an ear at night before bedtime.

There are also other women who contributed to archaeology but who are not included in this book for one of two reasons. First, *Ladies of the Field* is not intended to be an encyclopedic account of every female who in one form or another engaged with archaeology during the late nineteenth and early twentieth centuries. That would be a different kind of book—more a compilation of names and dates than a series of inspiring stories. Women such as Margaret Murray (1863–1963) who taught archaeology in the classroom more than they excavated in the field are not included here. Some women archaeologists, such as Edith Hall, were students of other earlier women archaeologists—in Hall's case, Harriet Boyd Hawes. Hence, some women's careers and contributions are folded into relevant chapters.

Second, some exceptional women archaeologists, such as Kathleen Kenyon (1906–1978), famous for her excavations at Jericho and first woman president of the Oxford Archaeological Society; Russia-born Tatiana Avenirovna Proskouriakoff (1909–1985), who conducted breakthrough work on Mayan hieroglyphics;

and even the German mathematician Maria Reiche (1903–1998), who spent her life surveying geoglyphs called the Nasca Lines in the Peruvian desert—all make their debuts just slightly after the period highlighted in this book: the Victorian era. Their lives and work are of great interest, but it was the earlier pioneers, the seven women discussed in chapters to follow, who paved their way.

The intent here is not to exclude (that has happened often enough to women's work throughout history) but rather to sharpen focus on seven lives that reveal much about early archaeology and what it took for women, in general, to become a part of it. The women presented here may have not been the very first to kick a shovel into the ground, but they were the first pioneering and fearless women who set upon archaeological research forcefully, unconventionally, and most of all, on their own terms. They worked in the field, excavating by themselves or in the company of hired teams and other female colleagues. They supervised ground-breaking excavations and made lasting contributions to archaeology as a growing science. Jane Dieulafoy and Agatha Christie worked alongside their husbands, but both enjoyed an uncommon degree of latitude in pursuing their own scholarly interests and were given credit for their expertise. Instead of "assistants," Dieulafoy and Christie were viewed by their spouses as true and equal partners.

Edwards, Bell, Christie, and Garrod were British; Dieulafoy, French; and Nuttall and Boyd Hawes, American. It's a Western team. Not one of the women presented here heralds from Asia or India, Africa or South America. That is because archaeology was born of Western science. It moved with spreading colonialism, was a tool of the British Empire, and fascinated the Western mind with its growing toolkit of physical evidence, theories, documentation, accurate measurements, hypothesizing, and overall propensity for logical explanation. This was a new way to interpret the past. The founders of archaeology were all of a Western European, and by extension, American mindset. It would be some time before other parts of the world began to systematically excavate their own backyards for history's buried remains.

In addition, the women chronicled here have all left handsome paper trails. Their journals, field notebooks, photographs, letters, diary entries, and publications allow a researcher to immerse herself in each woman's own historical context and tap into her spirit. It's the women who wrote enough to reveal themselves— their ambitions, frustrations, inspirations, and doubts—who made their way into this book. Based on the artifacts each woman left behind, could a pioneer and her legacy be brought into clear and compelling focus? Seven could, and these are the trendsetters who rode out into wide-open spaces, on horseback, donkey, or camel's hump, without precedent and against all odds to find what they were looking for.

THE ARCHAEOLOGICAL FIELD—DESERT dunes, riverbanks, crumbling ruins, and buried tombs—still exudes magnetism today. The romance of archaeology persists, and one has only to hum the tune of *Raiders of the Lost Ark* (duh-duh-duh-DUH! da-da-da!) and a scene of sweaty, dangerous adventure and jungle glory is unleashed. Yet aside from popular caricatures of archaeology, the passion for understanding human history—and more to the point, the story of what *makes us human*—is a quest that continually fascinates.

Sunken ships littered with skeletons and chandeliers, the fossilized footprints of an ancient ancestor in Africa, a bone amulet—these are the kinds of things archaeologists may find. Drawn to the tantalizing possibility that an ancient city, a site, or an artifact might be discovered that could change everything we thought we knew, we wait to see what comes next. Could there be a lost library containing thousands of books in a language never seen before? Perhaps a new link in the evolutionary chain of our species, a link with a wing nub instead of a shoulder blade? What if we find a buried wooden boat preserved in a bog that dates so far back that all the theories of human migration to the New World will need to be rewritten? Archaeology is uniquely, and consistently, able to renew and sometimes redefine our under-standing of ourselves.

As Amelia Edwards remarked in 1842, archaeology is that subject where "the interest never flags—the subject never stales—the mine is never exhausted."[8] Archaeology never stales because it keeps reinventing the big story of us.

The archaeological field is a centerpiece to each pioneer's story. Each woman found her way to some very out of the way places,

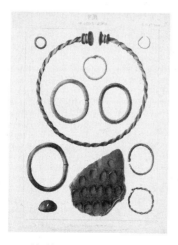 

LEFT: Necklace, bracelets, and fragment of decorated pottery
RIGHT: Earthenware vessel and stone artifacts

circa 1900, in the name of her research and study: Iraq, Iran, Crete, Morocco, Palestine, Syria, Gibraltar, Mexico. Often the field called to her with its own type of siren's song, a tune mingling mysteries of earth and history on a breeze. Today the field continues to beckon adventurous souls curious about where we've been and where we're going. The study of the past is nearly universal, and although each culture has a unique way of embracing and explaining its own history, archaeologists are a self-selecting crowd. They have their own particular, even peculiar toolkit and a strong desire to dig for history's precious leftovers.

Before the skies were filled with airplanes that could get you there and back, archaeology meant going off into strange places with only what a team could carry. Archaeologists would leave in search of something that *might* lie hidden beneath piles of dirt. Shovel in hand, they would chase that dream of discovery, becoming crazed and toilsome if it wasn't found, brilliant and cele-brated if it was. Despite its glamorous image, archaeology is hard work: dirty, muddy, sand-in-your-eyes, exhausting, inconvenient, and on occasion boring work. Not everyone's cup of tea, especially in the days of Victorian England when sipping tea was exactly what a lady was supposed to be doing.

Yet when they returned from the field, it was beyond dispute that the first women archaeologists had held their own physi-cally and intellectually in what was then a man's world. They had traveled, dug, scrutinized sites, managed, and made it. Impres-sive. So impressive that these women are sometimes in danger of being transformed into myth. Although I have boundless admira-tion for each of the women chronicled here, I try to avoid giving in to pure romanticism. The greatest honor is in keeping it honest. When you are working in the field you want your notes to be as accurate as possible, your maps as precise as can be, so that your reconstructions and interpretations are reliable. I aim for the same here. Legends can become the stuff of make-believe, overshadowing the realities and nuances of a true life.

These early archaeologists were never camelback saints (and they would be dull if they were). They were products of their time and made choices that by today's standards would elicit criticism and might even be judged as politically incorrect. In some cases they chose to play very much in a man's world and occasionally viewed other women, in popular patriarchal fashion, as dithering inferiors instead of comrades. They present sometimes frustrating contradictions that both support and undermine a feminist view. Complex individuals, they challenge us, as they once challenged their own peers and colleagues, to take them as they are.

With that in mind I ceremoniously opened an old archaeological field-journal of mine one breezy bayside day in northern California and invited the ladies in. *Come on down, drink coffee with me, spread your old maps out on my desk, and let's make a book together.* I asked them into my small studio, encouraged them to kick their dusty boots up onto the kitchen table. *Remind me of your crazy lives and courage.* I asked each of them to look over my shoulder as I wrote their respective chapters, and if that didn't make the writing any better, it did make my own journey through their stories richer.

Archaeology's essence is to uncover the origins of things, the epicenters of change, the evolution of style, technology, and everything else that makes us human. It makes sense that these pioneering women would take such a field of study as their own. As they challenged ideas about what a woman could accomplish, transformed styles of clothing through cross-dressing, cut their hair boyishly short, and broke into a scientific field previously denied them, little did the ladies know to what extent they were making history themselves.

ABOVE: Amelia Edwards, the revered godmother of Egyptology

AMELIA EDWARDS

. . . . .

THE NILE'S

Grand Dame

Sailing on the Nile, Amelia Edwards described her travels in a rented *dahabeeyah* (boathouse) as a "Noah's Ark life." It was a journey where the "sacred hawk" circling overhead uttered the "same sweet, piercing, melancholy note that the Pharaohs listened to of old," and it was to this accompaniment that her thoughts were swept up by the grandeur of bygone times. Other *dahabeeyahs* passed by hers, garlanded with crocodile skins and tourists, but Edwards remained aloof to other travelers and kept to her boat and crew, a team that exhibited "every shade of complexion from fair to dark, from tawny to copper-colour, from deepest bronze to bluest black."[1]

Her journeys through Egypt were mingled with history's ghosts and crowded with ancient ruins and temples, with the hieroglyphics inscribed on crushed potsherds and a quality of light that made the pyramids look like "piles of massy gold" at sunset. Drifting along the Nile, Edwards was in search of travel's pleasure as well as historical understanding. Yet what she ultimately found was to become her life's consuming passion: archaeology. This is the woman who would one day be heralded as the godmother of Egyptology.

Edwards was independent and financially secure from her career as a journalist and novelist. In her thirties, she packed her bags, left her English home, and let her sails fill with the breath of wandering. When she departed there was no one left in her life to advise against it; her parents had both recently died, and her only constant companion was a woman she referred to merely as "L."

By her own account, her later arrival in Egypt was almost by accident: ". . . without definite plans, outfit or any kind of Oriental experience, behold us arrive in Cairo on the 29th of November 1873, literally and most prosaically in search of fine weather."[2] Whether this is pure truth or a stylized start to her tale of discovery, the Egyptian Delta made its way firmly into her heart.

In all of her expeditions, Amelia was there to write. Tiptoeing on slopes "strewn with... fragments of mummy, shreds of mummy cloth, and human bones all whitening and withering in the sun,"[3] she recorded what she found and sketched the people she met. She was a travel writer, a tourist, a grand dame of the Nile, and she longed to make her own archaeological discovery.

One baking-hot afternoon a servant ran in with a penciled note, interrupting her lunch. It read: "Pray come immediately—I have found the entrance to a tomb." Breathless, Edwards ran to the scene of action. Dropping to her hands and knees, pushing her big skirts over her knees, shoveling sand with her bare hands, "heedless of possible sunstroke, unconscious of fatigue," she worked to excavate her first archaeological find. Pausing in her fast digging for just a moment, the Victorian lady pushed her hat back, sat on her heels, and turning to her companions asked, "If those at home could see us, what would they say!"[4]

BORN IN LONDON ON JUNE 7, 1831, Amelia Edwards—Amy to family and friends—was the only child in a family with modest means. Her mother, Alicia, was a "brilliant-complexioned, bright-eyed, large featured little Irish woman"[5] who home-schooled her daughter until the age of six and deliberately taught her nothing of domestic duty. Her mother must have thought lace patterns and buttons were a bore, and so she raised a daughter more comfortable in the library than near her mother's skirts. Edwards was one of the few girls in her day busy reading a book instead of learning to thread a needle. Mother and daughter were an active duo, as Alicia took her little girl out to cultural events and on boat trips. They spent a summer abroad in Ireland when Edwards was ten (Dad stayed home). It was during that trip that young Edwards first became fascinated with finding some "old round tower or ruined castle" and writing stories from the old-fashioned days when all was "love & fighting."[6]

Her father, Thomas Edwards, was a retired army officer and later a bank employee who, by the accounts available, seems to have been a little gloomy. A mildly depressed or absent figure—a slumpy silhouette reading in his study—he was quiet and removed in contrast to his vivacious wife and his daughter, who was already in possession of a fantastic imagination. Edwards's cousin Matilda described Mr. Edwards as a man whose "fireside influence was not inspiring" and a creature of "quiet, almost pensive habits."[7] As for Edwards, she only made a note when recalling childhood memories that her father's health was indifferent.[8]

As she grew up, Edwards made comic strips and books, combining her sketching skills with storytelling, and shared her work with family and friends, who encouraged her. Her first poem, "The Knights of Old," was composed when she was only seven and published in a local paper. By twelve she had a full story to her name. She continued writing stories and poems, later noting that "I was always writing or drawing, when other children were playing with dolls or dolls' houses." She thought herself a little lonely but was nevertheless content and absorbed by the world of words and history on which she thrived. As she entered her teens she began achieving recognition as both an accomplished artist (pencil sketching and watercolor were her fortés) and a performing musician who composed organ music. By the time she was in her mid-teens she was already determined to find and pursue her career, which she thought would be music.

Edwards had real talent and sang at concerts to ringing applause and flowers tossed to her feet. She wrote compositions that received flattering "testimonials" from the critics. She was even employed as an organist for a spell, and her career was seemingly launched. But she eventually realized that her musical abilities were good but not sublime. She knew that her genius lay elsewhere and suspected it might be lurking in the inkbottle. She got to writing and received her first payment, at age twenty-two, for the publication of her story "Annette" in 1853. Once she realized she could earn a living by words, her path forward was lit as if by blaze.

Writing became her life's purpose; it was her very nature. When interviewed about how she came to writing as a profession, Edwards explained her lifelong passion for it and even went so far as to take credit for having "anticipated the typewriter." Not for inventing it, just for having a hunch that a writing machine was coming. She had a gut feeling that technology would someday have to catch up with her prolific output.

Edwards's childhood hobby of creating poems and little stories steadily transformed itself into a life of journalism, literary essays, romantic tales, ghost stories, magazine articles, and surprisingly, for such an atypical Victorian woman, who some said couldn't even make a cup of tea, books on social etiquette and a ballroom guide. Her novels were widely recommended as great "railway reading," the equivalent of today's "good book for the plane," and they went through numerous editions and translations. She was finding success in print and,. for a woman of twenty-four years, significant financial independence to boot.

IN 1860, EDWARDS'S MOTHER AND FATHER died within a week of each other. They were hardly lovebirds, and it was odd as well as tragic that both parents should drop out of Edwards's life at the same time. She was only thirty when they died.

Edwards was without any real attachments at that point. She had a cousin she didn't get along with very well (also a writer, whom Edwards did *not* like to be confused with), and she was, technically, now a spinster. She had been briefly engaged nine years earlier but had found her suitor, Mr. Bacon, to be wanting. She noted that the engagement was not a happy one; they were ill suited and though Mr. Bacon proclaimed his love for Amelia, she could not genuinely reciprocate the feeling. She had accepted him out of esteem and a sense of duty and found these reasons insufficient to rationalize an entire life spent together. At least she was clear. She broke off their wedding plans with relief.

Being a free agent, perhaps much more so than she ever wished, Edwards went to live with old family friends, Mr. and Mrs. Braysher, in Kensington. The arrangement lasted the rest of her life until, almost ironically, thirty-two years later, Edwards and Mrs. Braysher died within weeks of each other.

After Mr. Bacon, Edwards never engaged a suitor again and never married. She didn't want to. She never felt romantic love for a man, though she did feel love, very much, for some of her women friends. Three women occupied her heart over the years: Marianne North, the famed botanical artist; Lucy Renshaw; and Kate Bradbury. One can only speculate whether or not Edwards was a lesbian (it does seem likely), but to be sure, she held her lady friends in very deep affection, loved them with devotion, and attributed much of her life's happiness to their companionship. To one, she gifted a gold ring. To another, she sent sketches addressed to her dear "poo Owl" and sometimes just to "Baby." A great sweetness in Amelia's life, perhaps the very greatest, was the women in her life.

Her friendship with Marianne North began shortly after the death of Edwards's parents and in mutual admiration—both women were independent, adventurous, clever, and accomplished. Yet over the course of a decade the relationship grew somewhat tortured for Edwards. The extent of her affection for North was not mutual, and it came to be seen by North as too much, too intense. Letters between the two women gathered in emotion and heat, revealing Edwards's desire to keep her friend close and the pullback from North as she gently dodged Edwards's reach and made plans to travel the world in search of exotic flowers to paint. Although the two did remain friends for life, stoking each other's fame and careers (almost politely), the intimacy of their friendship was diminished and Edwards was gutted by it. A phase of deep melancholy followed, and several illnesses slowed Edwards down. She entered a depression, one where in her darkest hours she lamented, "My heart no longer beats faster at the sight of a new or kindly & beautiful face. I hope nothing from it."[9] Melancholia haunted Edwards for much of her life. The arrival of her new friend "L" was, however, about to blow a giant new gale of happiness into things.

LUCY RENSHAW WAS the famous "L" mentioned in Edwards's travel accounts and books. Together, the two ladies embarked on some big adventures, beginning with Italy's famous Dolomites, a section of steep peaks in the Alps, and culminating in Egyptian sands. Edwards describes how they had "done some difficult walking in their time, over ice and snow, on lave cold and hot, up cinder-slopes and beds of mountain torrents…"[10] and they clearly shared an appetite for robust expeditions. Yet, in spite of all the frequent mention made of "L," Miss Renshaw is an unknowable figure. Details of her story are scant, some photographs of her are uncertain (in one—if it is indeed her—she's sporting short-cropped hair, a cravat, shadow-brushed sideburns, and a man's jacket![11]), and the things that can be said about her add up to simple summations. We know, for example, that Lucy was two years younger than Edwards; she sometimes wore a crimson shawl and according to Edwards was "given to vanities in the way of dress"[12]; she had a nurse's instinct; and she was very practical, capable, and certainly up for an adventure or two. She also liked to pet and feed the caged rabbits on board the *dahabeeyah*, all of which were awaiting their day in the kitchen pot. The details are slight; there's not much more to be had. Yet one thing does come into sharp focus thanks to Edwards's literary flair: Lucy and Amelia were the two women who had arrived fresh from Alexandria in 1873, after forty-eight hours of quarantine, to Shepherd's Hotel in Cairo:

> Where every fresh arrival has the honour of contributing, for at least a few minutes, to the general entertainment, the first appearance of L. and the Writer [Amelia Edwards], tired, dusty, and considerably sun-burned, may well have given rise to some comments in usual circulation at those crowded

tables. People asked each other, most likely, where these two wandering Englishwomen had come from; why they had not dressed for dinner; what brought them to Egypt; and if they were going up the Nile . . .[13]

The two disheveled ladies caused a stir, especially with sunburned faces in the age of creamy complexions. Famously, these lady travelers were in Egypt simply to find fair weather and cloudless skies. Edwards, however, was smart and knew how to shape her own tale. She was out to explore matters of archaeological interest too.

Under pale, hot skies, with a sketch pad in one hand, a parasol in the other, Edwards directed her crew and boat-bound companions to tour every archaeological site situated on the banks of the Nile. True to her Victorian sensibilities, she kept house in her *dahabeeyah*, the *Philae*—flowers always on the table, fresh brown bread to eat, tea in the afternoon, and a chaise longue on the deck; she rarely roughed it. Camelback rides were a thing designed, in her opinion, to kill a person; she had identified the four paces of a camel as: "a short walk, like the rolling of a small boat in a chopping sea; a long walk which dislocates every bone in your body; a trot that reduces you to imbecility; and a gallop that is sudden death." [14]

Edwards's appreciation of the Egyptian landscape is woven throughout the book that resulted from her travels up and down that glorious river, *A Thousand Miles Up the Nile*. Her account was a wild bestseller in the nineteenth century, and it's still in print today. She knew it was her best. In it she chronicles her days on the floating *dahabeeyah*, the open markets that smelled of cardamom and clove where a stall of bright red shoes was tucked beside withered old ladies in black robes. The women could tell

ABOVE: The Pyramids of Giza, circa 1890

you your fortune and sell you dates and oranges or perhaps sell you an entirely different fruit born of Egyptian soil: artifacts like fragments of pottery or pieces of bone.

Edwards portrays the pyramids in every shift of awe, wonder, and appreciation: "... the Great Pyramid in all its unexpected bulk and majesty towers close above one's head, the effect is as sudden as it is overwhelming. It shuts out the sky and the horizon."[15] Her words are painterly, luxuriant, sensuous, exemplified here by a description of sand wherein "the beauty of sand more than repays the fatigue of climbing it. Smooth, sheeny, satiny; fine as diamond-dust; supple, undulating, luminous, it lies in the most exquisite curves and wreaths, like a snowdrift turned to gold."[16] Elsewhere, "the towers we had first seen as we sailed by in the morning rose straight before us, magnificent in ruin, glittering to the sun, and relieved in creamy light against blue depths of sky. One was nearly perfect; the other shattered as if by the shock of an earthquake, was still so lofty that an Arab clambering from block to block midway of its vast height looked no bigger than a squirrel." [17]

Enchanted by the silks and spices of the bazaars, Edwards was equally repelled by the poorer villages and their "filthy, sickly, stunted and stolid" [18] residents, for whom she had genuine sympathy (comparing their circumstances to a situation "not worse . . . than in many an Irish village") but from whom she also wished to keep a "pleasant distance." As a British traveler she was more interested in Egypt's magnificent past (and the glorified imagination of it) than its relatively bedraggled present, where poverty was often extreme. Her observations of people and places were in accord with the times: Britain was civilized; other places, not so much. But unlike many who judged human civilization from the comfort of their armchairs, she was at least there to have a look. To form her own opinions. To see for herself. To learn and gauge what she could.

Edwards's comparison of a local man to a small "squirrel" reveals not just the size of the ruins, but also her attitude toward the locals, whom she was quick to dismiss and held in low esteem. They were not as "civilized" as she thought herself to be. Edwards's attitude wasn't confined to the local people, though. Throughout her tour, Edwards condescends to pretty much everyone on board the houseboat. Lucy is never referred to as more than "L." Edwards calls one of her fellow travelers the Little Lady, her new husband is the Idle Man, and another is known as the Painter. She never acknowledges the others' names or quite grants them status as real people in her book. At the same time, she refers to herself as the Writer and in crafting the travelogue was out to entertain as well as educate her reader.

All of the unnamed passengers have hobbies. One plans to hunt crocodiles for a parlor trophy, another to paint a "Great picture." Edwards's aim was to cultivate a keen knowledge of the ancient landscape around her. She became an expert on local archaeology while striding across lost ruins and crushing unseen potsherds underfoot. Starting in the North, the journey encompassed a remarkable one thousand miles of sailing. Edwards and her travel companions ventured to the very edge of *terra incognita*. They turned their giant riverboat around—a vessel approximately one hundred feet long by thirty feet wide—only upon reaching a vast section of unmapped country. Although Edwards was set on making new discoveries underfoot, she was less eager to get lost.

To start any Nile journey by heading south was an unusual choice. Because it was winter, most sailing would have to be done without the benefit of a strong tailwind or favorable currents. But traveling south gave Edwards more time to devour the books in her library, to become well versed in the landscape's antiquity, and to stop at each archaeological site on her northern return.

She carried Murray's *Handbook to Lower and Upper Egypt* like a Bible, and she meditated on how we look at the past. "It must be understood that we did not go to *see* the Pyramids," she muses. "We only went to *look* at them." [19] One involves active understanding, the other a more passive gaze, and Edwards ensured that she was knowledgeable about all historical relics that came before her. She would always "see" what was before her.

Much to the chagrin of her crew and companions, her wish for this voyage, based on historical sequence and personal preference, created long delays and extra sweat for everyone.

As they drifted south, Edwards drew the sites she saw. With a parasol in her gloved hand she even ventured into dark vaulted

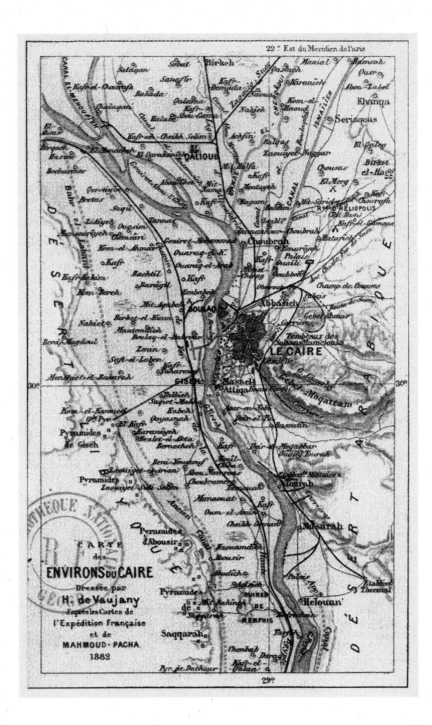

ABOVE: Map of Cairo and surrounding area, 1882

chambers and tombs to explore, following her local guide, who was carrying a lantern to light the way:

> So we went on, going every moment deeper into the solid rock, and farther from the open air and sunshine. Thinking it would be cold underground, we brought warm wraps in plenty; but the heat, on the contrary, was intense, and the atmosphere stifling... here for incalculable ages—for thousands of years probably before the Nile had even cut its path through Silsilis—a cloudless African sun had been pouring its daily floods of light and heat upon the dewless desert over head. The place might well be unendurable. It was like a great oven stored with the slowly accumulated heat of cycles so remote and so many that the earliest periods of Egyptian history seem, when compared with them, to belong to yesterday.[20]

For a lady of Victorian times, Edwards had no qualms about dark places and the unknown; it is not surprising that she wrote ghost stories for a living early in her career. Even dangerous river crossings held a thrill for her. The upper stretches of the Nile were, at that time, difficult to access because of the Aswan Cataract. Only the most skilled and brazen river captains would give it a go, and only the best of boats could hope to make it. A series of whirlpools and fast rapids, the cataract could take anywhere between twelve hours and four days to cross, and that was if the boat didn't smash into splinters. Although *Murray's Handbook* recommended that ladies watch the proceedings from the safety of the shore, Edwards took the helm. She wanted a front row seat and would have stayed there if she hadn't been lurched around so ferociously that she was obliged to move to the back. Because most tourists did not attempt the crossing, Edwards and group had the Nile more or less to themselves from there on out.

The silence they gained cast a new spell on Edwards. For her, the weight of history could now be felt more palpably in the sultry air. The imagination could fly a little more freely, soaring, as Edwards would often record, like the falcons of old did overhead. They were also moving toward the most anticipated archaeological site of all: Abu Simbel. Consisting of two massive stone temples built in the thirteenth century BC by the Pharaoh Rameses II as a monument to both his military might and his love for his wife, the queen Nefertari, the site was originally situated on the shores of Lake Nasser.[21] It was also physically elusive. Giant sand drifts would sometimes bury the site, leaving it only partially visible to those who had trekked so far to see it. At other times, the sands would blow away to reveal majestic rock carvings and hallowed entrances to painted rooms. Not knowing whether they would encounter the ancient monument exposed or hidden, Edwards was in appreciable suspense.[22]

Then, almost as if fate had played a hand in brushing aside the dunes and drifts, Edwards found a wonder. It was evening, and her first sighting of Abu Simbel arrived as a twilight dream:

> As the moon climbed higher, a light more mysterious and unreal than the light of day filled and overflowed the wide expanse of river and desert. We could see the mountains of Abou Simbel standing as it seemed across our path, in the far distance—a lower one first; then a larger; then a series of receding heights, all close together, yet all distinctly separate. That large one—the mountain of the Great Temple—held us like a spell. For a long time it looked like a mere mountain like the rest. By and by, however, we fancied we detected a

something—a shadow—such a shadow as might be cast by a gigantic buttress. Next appeared a black speck no bigger than a porthole. We knew that this black speck must be the doorway. We knew that the great statues were there, though not yet visible; and that we must see them soon. At length the last corner was rounded, and the Great Temple stood straight before us. The facade, sunk in the mountain side like a huge picture in a mighty frame, was now quite plain to see. The black speck was no longer a porthole, but a lofty doorway. Last of all, though it was night and they were still not much less than a mile away, the four colossi came out, ghostlike, vague, and shadowy, in the enchanted moonlight. Even as we watched them, they seemed to grow—to dilate— to be moving towards us out of the silvery distance.[23]

Edwards spent over a week investigating the site from morning to night and only agreed to depart as the complaints and impatience of her travel companions mounted. She made them promise that they could stop once again on the return home, and they did. Edwards's enchantment with Abu Simbel was profound; it was also the site of her own archaeological discovery. This was the place where she dropped to her knees in excavation.

The unexpected find was a small, square chamber where sand had gathered in a steep slope angled from the ceiling to the floor, lit by a lone sun shaft, and on every wall were painted friezes in bright unfaded color and bas-relief sculptures. She and the other travelers who excavated by her side correctly surmised that the place had never been discovered. Edwards quickly had the ship crew working like "tigers" and sent someone to the nearest village to hire another fifty hands to help. The excavation was underway and "... the sand poured off in a steady stream like water." When

ABOVE: A Victorian lady traveler assisted by local men

all had been cleared away, Edwards, the Painter, and even the Idle Man gathered in the chamber and got busy copying inscriptions, measuring and surveying the find, sketching the walls, and sniffing around for any further surprises. It was at that moment that the Idle Man lifted a human skull from the sand.

Could a tomb be underfoot? Were mummies and papyri and jewels only a shovel scoop away? A smaller skull appeared next, one as "pure and fragile in texture as the cup of a water-lily."[24] Everyone must have been holding their breath, hearts racing with the thought of a spectacular, gold-covered, ruby-lit, hieroglyphics-laden find.

Unfortunately, the new room proved to be only an empty basement. All archaeological hopes were dashed. What they had found in the decorated room, however, was apparently a lost library. Even if the discovery wasn't as grand as the group had hoped, Edwards took special pride in it. It was a turning point for her, the moment when archaeology became not just a subject of study but a personal experience.

Lifting fragile old bones from the earth and brushing sand away from ancient objects were no longer activities that belonged to someone else, no longer the remote and exciting discoveries one read about in a book or newspaper article, actions that seemed exciting yet inaccessible. Edwards could now experience the thrill of unearthing a small piece of history with her own two hands. Archaeology was no longer a dream or a distant desire: it had become real.

With that feeling came a heightened awareness of archaeology's value and its vulnerability. Shoveling sand, she was dismayed to see that workmen "wet with perspiration" were leaning against the paintings, marring their brilliance and smearing the color. She felt conflicted when the Painter scratched their names and the date of the chamber's discovery into the ancient walls. That was a normal practice back then, but it nonetheless soiled the purity of the place. As Edwards thought about all the artifacts for sale at roadside stalls, the museum collections where prized objects had been stolen from their place, the common looting, and the slow deterioration and loss of some of the world's greatest historic sites, she was struck by the unshakable desire to do something about it. A bolt of passion. A call to arms. She would appeal to her readers with a question:

> I am told that the wall paintings which we had the happiness of admiring in all their beauty and freshness are already much injured. Such is the fate of every Egyptian monument, great or small. The tourist carves it over with names and dates, and in some instances with caricatures. The student of Egyptology, by taking wet paper "squeezes" sponges away every vestige of the original colour. The "Collector" buys and carries everything off of value that he can, and the Arab

steals it for him. The work of destruction meanwhile goes on apace ... The Museums of Berlin, of Turin, of Florence are rich in spoils which tell their lamentable tale. When science leads the way, is it wonderful that ignorance should follow?[25]

JUMPING AHEAD eight years, Edwards is a woman out of the field and at her desk. Returned to her life in England, she sits in her personal library, which contains over three thousand books. Littered on the shelves and lined up in tall cases are specimens of Greek and Etruscan pottery, Egyptian antiquities, antique glass, engravings, and watercolor sketches. She's a matronly woman, robust and smart looking, silver hair swept up and braided on top of her head, eyes dark and intelligent, her features rather beautiful. Outside the wild birds are in a tizzy, and "thrushes drop fearlessly into the library to be fed," while the robins perch on the tops of high books and at Edwards's feet as she lies "reading or writing in a long Indian chair under a shady tree" on a summer day.[26] She has since her travels along the Nile become a reputable Egyptologist in her own right. Edwards has taught herself to read hieroglyphics—a mighty task. She has also redirected her passion for Egypt's archaeology into something of a savior's work.

Passions still simmering, Amelia Edwards was the woman responsible for thinking of, advocating for, and ultimately assembling the Egypt Exploration Fund, which was later renamed the Egypt Exploration Society.[27] A powerful organizer, she led the way in promoting research and excavation in the Nile Delta. As the society notes in its own organizational history, "Amelia Edwards, together with Reginald Stuart Poole of the Department of Coins and Medals at the British Museum, founded the Egypt Exploration Fund in 1882 in order, as announced at the time in several daily newspapers, 'to raise a fund for the purpose of conducting excavations in the Delta, which up to this time has been very rarely visited by travellers.'" In asking the public for financial contribution, she enabled a host of new investigations and played a critical role in the whole enterprise of Egyptology. Most notably, she was instrumental in recruiting a young archaeologist named Sir Flinders Petrie to her cause.

Petrie would come to be known as the father of modern archaeology. Why? Because he kept the small stuff. Whereas most archaeologists of the day pursued trophy finds, destroying valuable evidence in their hunt to obtain friezes and sculptures for European museums, Petrie recognized the inherent worth of the potsherds, fragmentary inscriptions, and broken utilitarian wares from the past. This was the stuff of everyday life, which could provide a sequential understanding of historic events. Petrie developed a dating method still used by archaeologists today called seriation, which relies on relative comparison. A style of pottery is associated with a particular time period. Once that is established, chronologies can be determined for sites and for all the different artifacts types found within. Petrie's method constituted the best of scientific field archaeology available until the advent of radiocarbon dating in the mid-twentieth century.

At her desk, Edwards rewrote Petrie's field journals into popular articles so that the public could understand and appreciate the significance of his findings. It was this unique collaboration that helped give the London-based Egypt Exploration Fund an international reputation. As honorary secretary and the tireless recruiter of new subscribers, Edwards was the force behind one of archaeology's great men and most productive societies.

She saw her work with the fund as absolutely worthwhile, worthy of her talents, and most of all, necessary. It not only guaranteed new excavations and research but also helped safeguard antiquities and raise public awareness of the threats faced by fragile cultural relics. Edwards handwrote thousands of letters every year, imploring (she would say "begging") people to support the effort. She oversaw the publication of all archaeological reports and news. Over time her duties grew bigger and more administrative, and she was stretched thinner. Exhausted by the work involved, and by some of the brackish personalities she had to reckon with to get anything accomplished, she began to tire. She was no longer writing novels, and her finances took a nosedive. When Petrie complained about the incompetence of the fund and threatened to leave, she let him have it:

> I have given the best part of 7 years to it. My time, I admit, is not scientifically so valuable as yours . . . But *in the market* my time is worth a great deal more than yours. [Her novels paid handsomely, and she had turned down two offers to write new ones.] It is madness perhaps on my part to desire to preserve my chains unbroken—& yet I wd fain see the work go on; that work wh. is glory to you & Mr. Naville—& poverty & obscurity for me.[28]

She felt as though she had disappeared behind a mountain of letters, publications, and messages, her own success as a bestselling author eclipsed by the everyday needs of supporting archaeology. She couldn't even take comfort in the fact that her own skills in reading hieroglyphics were so highly regarded that experts sent samples of potsherds and papyrus to her for translation. Edwards's fingers were cramped from composing too many letters, and her bank account was circling the drain.

In spite of this hardship, Edwards was *the* voice for Egyptology. Her knowledge of the field was vast and expert, and she was about to emerge from whatever obscurity she felt to face the world in an unprecedented manner. She had a plan, a big one. But first there was Kate. Kate Bradbury was the energetic thirty-four-year-old woman who doted on Edwards and looked after her. It was because of this trusted bond (and the need for some money) that Edwards embarked on an ambitious lecture series in America in 1889. With Kate there to help her, she put her strong understanding of current archaeology in Egypt into motion and claimed a piece of the fame that was deservedly hers.

With jittery nerves and a streak of genuine panic, Edwards still proved to be a public-speaking phenomenon. Her lectures weren't attended by just a handful of spectacle-wearing, gray-haired men; thousands came, both because of Edwards's reputation as a scholar and because of the public's fascination with the subject. Over two thousand people attended her first lecture, titled "The buried cities of ancient Egypt."[29] Reporters rushed to greet her; newspapers announced her arrival in each city; ladies' societies and other organizations welcomed her to their luncheons as a celebrity. A collection of her lectures makes up the book *Pharaohs, Fellahs and Explorers* (1891), published posthumously.

Just as her writing combined scholarship with wit and an easy narrative, Edwards's lectures simultaneously entertained and educated. This was always the beauty of her work. Probably her greatest contribution to archaeology was that of "bridge." She was the mechanism that connected field experience and the solid understanding of a science and its achievements with the enviable twist of popular appeal. What made her books sell is the same thing that made people subscribe in droves to the Egypt Exploration Fund. Edwards had the rare gift of making archaeology not only accessible to the general public, but also absolutely fascinating.

THE AMERICAN LECTURE tour schedule was demanding. Even by today's travel standards, she was on a circuit that would exhaust anyone: 120 lectures in less than a year. Kate was beat, and Edwards seemed to be running on the fumes of glory alone. Things began to slow down for her when she fell and broke her arm and soon afterwards began a battle with breast cancer. She underwent a successful operation to remove the malignant tumor, but her health declined anyway. Edwards continued to lecture even as her health dwindled. Each new lecture offered a chance to spark renewed vigor, but Edwards couldn't keep it up. She died in April 1892.

By the time of her death Edwards had been awarded three honorary degrees, from Columbia University, Smith College, and the College of the Sisters of Bethany in Topeka, Kansas. Her will stipulated that her entire library and all of her artifacts, engravings, sketches, and more should go to support the Edwards Chair of Egyptology. To this end she also gave £5,000 (a fortune then) to fund the Chair at University College London and made clear whom she wanted to be appointed. The recipient had to be under the age of forty, and so no one working at the British Museum could be considered for the role. In this way, Edwards cleverly guaranteed that only Flinders Petrie could get the job.[30] Meanwhile, her cherished Kate, her "poo Owl," went on to marry a professor of Egyptology at Oxford University, Francis Llewellyn Griffith. With Edwards as her mentor, one has to wonder who had the better conversation: the professor or his very learned wife.

WHAT WAS IT about archaeology, and more specifically Egyptology, that attracted Edwards so strongly? She had a successful career and, had she desired it, could have written romance novels until she was old and gray, made loads of money, traveled widely, seen it all. With her appetite for adventure, Edwards might have made a whole life out of simply traveling the world, observing first-class digs, checking off a list of archaeological sites to visit like groceries to buy. Instead, she decided to get involved. She fought for archaeology, for its development, expansion, and cause.

Her instinct for archaeology can be traced back to her girlhood desire to write about bygone times when all was "love & fighting." Amelia Edwards was a romantic. For her, the past was a great canvas and archaeology her palette. Her imagination could move all over that canvas—spanning thousands of years—filling it in with detail and antiqued color, sketching people, events, and monuments of wondrous, sacred quality. As a writer, Edwards approached archaeology through a highly emotional lens. In the beginning she chose archaeology as a way of life because the ancient world provided a backdrop to the stories she loved most. Ancient Egypt was home to pharaohs and kings. A lost time. A day of golden tombs and falcons. She reveled in it.

Later that love grew into something more concrete, a little less fanciful. Edwards's fascination with archaeology moved towards a concerted effort to preserve the past. To lose evidence of Egypt's history—that beauty she both saw and imagined—or to leave pieces of it buried and poorly excavated, was a crime she could not condone. Amelia Edwards, grand dame of the Nile, uniquely embodied romance and practicality in her approach to history's ruins. Without her, archaeology might have remained as dry as the very bones it unearths.

ABOVE: Dieulafoy, famous for her cross-dressing, easily and often mistaken for a young man

JANE DIEULAFOY

· · · · ·

In a Man's Suit

air cropped mannishly short, a board strapped beneath her white linen shirt, and a red ribbon looped through the buttonhole of her well-cut suit jacket, Jane Dieulafoy embraced *la vie de l'homme*. In a day when new brides were expected to tuck into homemaking, to fluff the nest and prepare for babies to arrive, the Dieulafoys began their marriage in a radically different way. Shortly after their wedding, Jane Dieulafoy dressed herself convincingly as a boy and fought as a front-line solider alongside her husband, Marcel, during the Franco-Prussian war of 1870. She camped with the men, never revealing her identity as a woman, and trekked with the army of the Loire through harsh conditions and definite danger.

Later, as her interest in archaeology blossomed and her explorations in the field took her to what is now Iran, she adopted the dress of a western man completely. Forsaking the ruffled petticoat, Dieulafoy was one of the first European women to slip into a pair of pants. In doing so she became something of celebrity in nineteenth-century Paris where she was both admired and mocked. She never went back to women's clothing. Her cross-dressing had something of a Charlie Chaplin effect; she looked a touch comic in pictures and sketches yet completely put together and fashionable, her shirt buttoned high up her neck, waistcoat snug, trousers perfectly tailored, black shoes laced and polished.

Through her writings, personal and published, it's evident that Dieulafoy was bored by Victorian society. She longed to "pass the days and ease the burden"[1] of the bourgeois life she was born into, and only upon returning from exhausting field excavations did she allow herself to be fêted by salon society. Hardships of the field were washed away with disinfectant soap and champagne, while the artifacts she and Marcel acquired abroad significantly enriched the collections of the Louvre Museum. Perhaps one of their most famous finds, the Lion Frieze at Susa, spurred both public wonder and long ticket lines. Its discovery was something of a miracle after weeks of bad weather and poor luck.

When she wasn't on site, Dieulafoy was a prolific travel writer. By virtue of her pen, she was able to leave Parisian life and daily humdrum to roam desert dunes and ancient tells again. She invited the men and women of France to join her on those journeys, bringing the exoticism of the Orient and the feel of camelback sojourns into their reading rooms. Her life of adventure is what led the *New York Times* to refer to her as the lady "regarded as the most remarkable woman in France and perhaps in all of Europe."[2]

Tough, strong-willed, highly singular, Dieulafoy was by her own definition a "collaborateur" with her archaeologist husband, Marcel. She deliberately chose the masculine form of the French word to convey her meaning. No "la" here. Yet what was there was ... *l'amour.*

Almost as fascinating as Dieulafoy's unorthodox way of life was her marriage. The relationship she and Marcel formed was built on professional respect, partnership, equality, and affection in a time when these qualities were rare in a marriage. Dieulafoy reminds us that being an accomplished and daring woman in her time didn't require a dismissal of the other half. A woman could be a daredevil *and* married. For unlike some of the other pioneers in this book, she found an outlet for her explorations, intellect, and professional pursuits as a highly regarded and beloved partner.[3] Marcel publicly acknowledged her work and her partnership when most women and their contributions, scientific and otherwise, were greeted with silence or at best a slight mention. Even today's feminist scholars acknowledge that the Dieulafoys had something special going on.

Jane Dieulafoy was a commendable archaeologist and a real first in the field. Her crews, all men, numbered in the hundreds, and she often oversaw them by herself. Beneath desert skies, inland and away from water, having suffered months of sterile digging—where each shovelful of dirt comes up empty, high hopes for a find decrease, and motivation weakens—Dieulafoy remained steadfastly devoted to her purpose. More than a treasure-hunter, she was very much the burgeoning scientist with a clear objective: the site of Susa. Monitoring the excavation trenches, devising field methods when there were few to none established, and meticulously mapping, labeling, and reconstructing what was discovered, Dieulafoy gave archaeology a good name. She gave "woman" a good name too, even if it was all dressed up in a man's suit.

JANE DIEULAFOY WAS born Jane Henriette Magre in Toulouse on July 29, 1851. Her parents were well off, a family of bourgeoisie merchants that owned two countryside properties where Dieulafoy grew up as a "small, slender and blond" girl who "lacked neither grace nor charm."[4] Dieulafoy's father died when she was very young, and she and her five siblings grew up under the care of their mother. Jane was bright and intelligent, a girl described as both mocking and affectionate. She was possessed of a quick wit and was already marching to a different beat from that of most little girls her age. Dieulafoy's mother enrolled her daughter in a convent, the Couvent de l'Assomption d'Auteuil in Paris, at age eleven so that she would have an above-average education. There she was instructed by the sisters in Latin and Greek and lived a life of very strict routine and schedule: early mornings, prayers before breakfast, cleaning, studying, more prayers, bedtime. She didn't rebel against this routine but, as she did for all of her life, accepted the very conventional conditions and even adhered to them with gusto and conviction. Yet she still managed to turn every assumption and rule on its head.

She stayed at the convent until she was nineteen years old and, a little surprisingly given her nonconformist stance on most matters later on, moved straight into marriage. Her charms, and a "face always crinkled in a smile,"[5] caught hold of Marcel Dieulafoy's heart. Marcel was a well-traveled young man, an engineer who specialized in railways, and he had a handsome face tanned by travels in Africa. Like Jane's, his family also lived in Toulouse. Both families were well off, influential, and likely acquainted. From the cool confines of the convent, with its musty books and pursuits in spiritual atonement, Dieulafoy must have been gripped with excitement to meet a man who promised so much in the way of warmth and new direction. He was the open door to both opportunity and the Orient. She accepted his marriage proposal quickly, and thus began a life of partnership that would last forty-six years—until death did make them part.

Schooling complete, a comfortable marriage at just the right age, Dieulafoy moved through society smoothly and appropriately, with little upset. But with Marcel now by her side, the two jointly threw open the doors of life and considered a scene of vast possibility. Dieulafoy was powerfully committed to Marcel, not so much as a "wife" in the traditional Victorian sense of service and submission, but as a fiery life partner. As was Marcel to her. And they would make the very most of life.

During the Franco-Prussian War of 1870, when French forces began to buckle under the power of the Prussians and enemy ranks laid siege around the very walls of Paris, Marcel became furious. He requested active service (no draft or obligation to military service was in place) and was enlisted as a captain in command of troops based in the town lyrically named Nevers. When he went to war, Dieulafoy did too. A bride of barely twenty, she donned her first pair of gray trousers and a soldier's overcoat, disguising herself as a boy—a clean-shaven sharpshooter, to be exact.

Women were only allowed to join the army as canteen workers. They dished food and filled water cups. Whether it was for love of Marcel or for an equally passionate drive to protect her motherland, Dieulafoy didn't hesitate to choose the rifle over a soup ladle and become a warrior. She and Marcel endured a terrible winter together of marches, hunger, and exhaustion. Although cheered by their comrades' acts of heroism, they were depleted, emotionally and physically, by the grisly horrors of war. Their bizarre honeymoon was spent on the violent frontlines. When it was over the Dieulafoys returned home, discouraged because their effort had not been victorious, but back in Toulouse they resumed a relatively normal life. Marcel went back to work, and Dieulafoy likely buttoned herself back into petticoats.

Domestic stability was nothing either craved, however. They were both intrigued by the exotic lands of the East; for Marcel they held special architectural interest. He believed that Western medieval architecture had its roots in the ornate styles found in the ancient mosques and buildings of the Orient, and his quest to prove this supposition began to define his chief interests. He wasn't an archaeologist by training, but he was by nature. The Dieulafoys left France every year for trips to Egypt and Morocco, where they traced architectural influences and began to knit their passion for travel and historical research together. By 1880 they were preparing for their biggest adventure yet: Persia. This was where Dieulafoy said her husband would seek "the link which connects Oriental art with that of Gothic art," the phenomenon that, "sprang so suddenly in the Middle Ages..."[6]

MEN'S CLOTHES WERE comfortable, pants were much better than skirts, and boots and overcoats were much more practical than dainty shoes and lacy gloves. After growing fond of men's attire during the war, Dieulafoy probably didn't even bother to pack a dress for Persia. An article from 1894 describes the Dieulafoys as a couple who "agree that a common *dress* enables man and wife to submit to the same conditions and share the same pursuits. One can go where the other goes in bad weather. Vicissitudes of travel and arbitrary social rules that make distinctions for petticoats are effaced. It permits an unbroken companionship. It makes possible one life where there are two lives."[7]

United by love and two pairs of trousers, Jane and Marcel spent a full year planning for their excursion to Persia, a trip that would last nearly twenty-four months. They departed in 1881, and upon

Madame Dieulafoy. — Dessin de É. Bayard, d'après une photographie.

ABOVE: Jane Dieulafoy, age thirty, dressed for travel and hard work in the field

arrival in Persia they started to travel by horseback, carrying bags filled with photography equipment: cameras, glass plates, chemicals, and such. They also carried weapons. Two westerners—seemingly two *men* by anyone's quick glance—without escort were very vulnerable to attack from unfriendly strangers. The Dieulafoys traveled an extraordinary 3,700 miles in the saddle between 1881 and 1882.[8] As they moved across the landscape, they systematically documented and photographed old buildings along the way, creating a treasure trove of reference material for generations of future historians and archaeologists.

Their "unbroken companionship" was put to a test that would sink many couples. There were days of pummeling rain, bad fevers all around, nights spent sleeping on rocky floors, stretched financial resources, and, for Jane Dieulafoy, a head full of lice and hair that she had to continually shave. Her blond locks gone, she

LEFT: Ancient glassware recovered intact from an archaeological site
RIGHT: Ornately carved spoons and ceramic bowls

looked just like a young man, "a rifle on her shoulder and a whip in her hand," and one of her biographers explains that "she fooled everyone, from robbers on the highways to the shah himself, who did not want to believe her when she revealed her actual gender."[9]

Throughout their travels the goal was always a remote and legendary place called Susa. Situated at a distance east of the Tigris River, the Susa region was home to an ancient city that had already undergone some cursory excavation years before. The Dieulafoys knew that its potential was great, and they wanted to have a hand in uncovering the ruins. All of that would come later though.

Their journey to Susa was strenuous, and both were sick and worn down by the time they arrived in a deluge of heavy rain. After nonstop travel, saddle burn, and months of camping, they must have craved a clean, comfortable bed. Perhaps even some croissants and a current copy of *Le Tour du Monde*. Having made the acquaintance of Susa, they left knowing that they would be back. Dieulafoy wrote in her notebook, "The *souvenir* of Susa haunted my husband in his sleep."[10]

SUSA WAS AN ancient town surrounded by what was then a widespread emptiness: "... there is not a single habitation to enliven the landscape. Some nomad Persians and Arabs camp in this vast solitude, and live wild and savage on the milk of their herds, or on the fruits of plundering raids,"[11] explained Jane through her nineteenth-century looking glass. As a royal city, Susa once exerted an influence greater than that of Babylon, and it was a town of "radiant focus" where artists from as far away as Greece would gather, flourish, create.

When the Dieulafoys returned to Susa in 1884—now on site to properly excavate and with all permissions secured as well as a formal team to begin work—they stood before an artificial mountain and a series of hills technically known as "tells." It was a landmass created by thousands of years of earth and wind quietly cooperating to bury a city. Crumbling palace towers were peaks, and ancient roads had become low valleys where "wild cats and boars" roamed. Dieulafoy was bursting with happiness at their arrival: "The weather was rainy; our tents let in the moisture; provisions were short; our soup cooked in the open air, was better provided with rain water than with butter; nevertheless we were joyous—joyous because we had reached Susa, joyous because we had taken possession of the site which we had so long aspired to excavate."[12]

The team unloaded their pickaxes, buckets, and tools and then, with enthusiasm still pouncing, faced three small dilemmas: the first, where to start? Choosing where the first trench should go was like opening the pages of a coverless book, hoping it was the one you wanted in a library's line up of thousands. Would they plant their shovel right? Find something fast, or sift sand that contained nothing at all? Second, they had no workmen and they would need scores. And third, everything they excavated was under the watchful eye of locals who believed, perhaps rightfully so, that the artifacts belonged to them, not the Dieulafoys. The dunes were alive with these looters in search of golden relics, and come nightfall they would try to raid the site.

In deciding where to start, the team considered the work of excavations conducted thirty years earlier by two British men. Based on their preliminary findings, the Dieulafoys had a rough sense of where column bases and even a helpful inscription or two were located. The team decided to take their chances and excavate three tells all at once. These consisted of a throne room, the citadel, and a private residence called the "King of Kings."[13]

With the massive digging task before them, they turned to the locals for help in recruiting a veritable army of workers. In her notes, Jane laughs at the process whereby "an old Arab, whose only nourishment consisted of the herbs which he browsed on the tumulus [an archaeological mound, or tell], a poor devil who had been robbed by the nomads, and the son of a widow who was dying of starvation in the Gabee, were at last enrolled at fancy prices... Marcel and myself took command of this glorious battalion."[14] It was a modest start, but the ranks of their field crew would eventually swell to more than three hundred men.

News of the excavations carried far and wide, and eventually their biggest headache was too much help. Crowds of men wanted to work the trenches. Every morning at the crack of dawn they would surge to the site, spades in hands, and if not put to use and given a day's wage, they became surly and tried to "pillage the tents." Once a desolate spot in the desert, the Dieulafoys had transformed Susa into a hub of swarming bodies—shoveling, sweating, and sorting.

As for the nightly danger of looters, that was solved simply: firearms. Armed watchmen were installed around the site and paid a fee more lucrative than theft. It was with all this in place that Jane Dieulafoy stood up tall, walked to the trench, and grabbed hold of her tools for the first breaking of ground (a little like smashing a champagne bottle in celebratory spirit). She captures the moment: "Full of emotion, I struck the first blow with the pick on the Achaemenidaen tumulus, and worked until my strength gave out... this was how the excavations at Susa were begun."[15]

The trenches grew deep quickly, but they were achingly empty. Fourteen feet of nothing. A few funeral urns were found here and there, each with a skeleton curled up inside, but aside from that the dirt was barren. Rain continued to pour, and the team stood mired in tacky mud, working long hours all day with only two things to look forward to: a wet tent and hope for tomorrow's discovery. This was the stuff of typical field archaeology. For each day of glory and spectacular finds there are long weeks— and sometimes entire seasons—of toil and tedium.

Luckily for the team, Dieulafoy soon had cause to shout, "Heaven be praised!"

One of the workmen had scraped the surface of some bricks glazed in colorful enamel. The workers redirected the trenches and opened them wide: two hundred feet long and twenty-six feet across. A month of careful excavation followed, and they were rewarded with the find of a lifetime: the Lion Frieze. They assembled this ancient masterpiece, fragment by bright fragment, on the floor of their tent. It was by Dieulafoy's own account "magnificent," with each lion measuring more than eleven feet long. Dieulafoy wrote of her find: "The animal stands out against a turquoise blue background; the body is white, the head surrounded by a sort of green victorine, the mustache blue and yellow, the flanks white, the belly blue. In spite of its extravagant coloration the beast has a terribly ferocious aspect." [16]

The Lion Frieze ushered in a new pace of discovery. Soon there was an opal seal in Dieulafoy's hand that belonged to Xerxes the Great, along with carved ivory, spear heads, bottles, bronze and terra-cotta lamps, engraved stones, coins, funeral urns, and a "thousand interesting utensils." A life-size painting of a black man in rich robes was revealed and left the crew to ponder whether they were in the company of the ancient Ethiopians Homer once spoke of. In fact, much of what they uncovered let their minds run with theories and speculation about the ancient world. This was not a single dwelling or cave they were exploring; it was a cultural epicenter, a whole city. The Dieulafoys and team scraped away all they could to shine a light on the region's sprawling past.

MIDWAY THROUGH THE excavations at Susa the Dieulafoys had accumulated so much cargo that they had to figure out how to transport it out of the country. There were fifty-four wooden boxes filled to the brim, and everything that didn't fit in those was buried by night in a secret spot known only to the Dieulafoys.[17] Anxious to avoid a two-hundred-mile-long journey through a country where the objects they had collected were viewed as "belonging of the prophet" and therefore "treasures and talismans" that the locals would (naturally) want back, they made a dash for Turkey. An etching titled "Transporting Treasures Across The Jungle From Susa To The Persian Gulf" depicts seventeen villagers heaving a single cargo box through tall grass by rope. Their effort wasn't helped by two men in pith helmets (or could it be Jane sitting beside Marcel?) who sat lounging on *top* of the cargo the workers were shouldering.[18]

Once they reached the Turkish coast they breathed a sigh of relief, only to find that customs officials wanted thousands of francs in exchange for the cargo's unblocked passage; the Dieulafoys' plan for an easy exit was ruined. If the money wasn't forthcoming, customs suggested that the treasures of Susa might sit nicely in the museum of Constantinople. The situation was precarious.

Through delicate negotiation, the Dieulafoys managed to have the boxes stored in Bassorah, while the French consul tried to solve the messy situation diplomatically. Like parents unwilling to let their children out of sight, Jane and Marcel camped by their crates of artifacts. Dieulafoy described the intensity of their predicament: "we were kept continually under strict watch, while gun-boats cruised in the river with orders to sink us if the slightest attempt at escape was made."[19]

In the end, they had to leave their cargo and wait patiently for matters to be solved through political forces. That would take at least a year. Jane and Marcel packed their bags, sneaking a lion's head and small objects into their personal luggage, and returned to France for a visit.[20]

As soon as they could, however, they returned to Susa to conclude their work. When they arrived back on site they were greeted by hundreds of workmen already there and eager to get back to it. Excavations resumed as if they had never been interrupted. More stunning finds were soon made, including the Frieze of Archers and the Palace of Darius. "One day we discovered a hand, the next day a foot shod with a golden boot; finally the enamels became abundant." The archers were in a marching procession so grand and handsome they could compete with the lions still marooned in Turkey. Throughout all of this, Dieulafoy was at the center of the action: overseeing the workmen, watching the trenches, and organizing the "daily harvest of enameled bricks,"[21] each of which needed to be cleaned, labeled, and packed perfectly for future reconstruction.

Her delight in the excavation's results is made plain in all she wrote about it. For her, there was a steady stream of optimism in spite of workdays that started at 4:30 AM and never quite ended (evenings in the tent were devoted to note taking, strategy, artifact analysis, and the piecing together of broken pots). During her time at Susa, Dieulafoy endured every fist the field could throw, from foul weather to sterile excavations to dangerous attacks from raiders, and still she writes about the site's fruitful excavations in a breezy style. For Dieulafoy, uncovering the wealth of Susa was deeply satisfying, and she came to know her

ABOVE: Jane Dieulafoy protecting her crates of precious artifacts against theft

way through the trenches of an ancient city much better than any kitchen or tea parlor.

ANOTHER, MORE EXTENDED return to France was inevitable and probably even anticipated with some relief. The Dieulafoys returned as archaeological celebrities, and the sum of all their fieldwork could now be written up and published. Both of them were also wracked by fever, and a hot bath must have been a blessing. They had amassed four hundred crates of archaeological material (forty-five tons in weight[22]), all of which would be delivered straight to Paris via ship and rail. The Lion Frieze would eventually make its way unharmed to the Louvre too.

During her time at Susa, Dieulafoy wore men's clothes exclusively. A photo taken of her while in the field shows a woman who, no matter how carefully one scrutinizes the picture, looks just like a man.[23] She sits on a small cot, large umbrella in the corner, facing the two men in her company. Her legs are parted, not crossed, and she's resting her cheek in her hand, a pose that is tough and shows her ease in a field camp. She looks impatient, likely because the rain is pouring outside and keeping her from her work. Her outfit is the daily standard: black leather boots, dark pants that appear thick and heavy like wool, a man's shirt buttoned up to the neck, and a man's overcoat, no collar, buttons down the front, cuffs turned. Her hair is short as a schoolboy's and she sports a plain black hat on her head. Coffee cups are strewn about, and at her feet are a number of kettles and containers, each hand-drawn in the photo and touched up with what looks like dabs of whiteout and blue ink. Piles of saddles, field gear, blankets, and boxes surround Dieulafoy and her companions. One of the fellows is smoking a hookah in the corner; the other, with very short dark hair, black eyes, and a mustache, is looking away absently. Rugs are spread on the ground and hay beneath that. A thin tree trunk in the center holds the tent up, and its fabric radiates behind Dieulafoy in a sweeping fan of vertical lines that evoke just a hint of circus tent. She is clearly in her element.

Upon her return to Paris, Dieulafoy publicly forsook women's clothing completely and forever. She explained her decision to dress in masculine attire as something she did for comfort and practicality: "I only do this to save time. I buy ready-made suits and I can use the time saved this way to do more work." [24] But surely, she was also aware of its effect and must have enjoyed the sensation she created.

For Dieulafoy, wearing men's clothes was not the equivalent of wearing sweats or her husband's sweater around the house (or the site). She wore up-to-the-minute Parisian men's fashion for all it was worth. Jane Dieulafoy was a genuine cross-dresser. While an overcoat had afforded her disguise as a boy during the

Franco-Prussian War, her dress now had nothing to do with deception or safety; rather, it was a bold and personal statement. She even had to get police permission to dress as she did. *The New York Times* reported on the illustrious Madame Dieulafoy, who, "having become accustomed to wearing man's clothing during her travels, received the authorization of the Government to appear in public in the costume."[25] This privilege was normally reserved only for the ill or handicapped.

It was a personal statement, but what kind? Beyond comfort and "practicality," was there another meaning? Some have ventured that Dieulafoy was a lesbian, a nineteenth-century butch of sorts. Yet her love for and partnership with Marcel was very profound and seemingly romantic too. There is no evidence that she was ever with other women. And quite at odds with the notion of lesbianism at the time, Dieulafoy was extremely conservative. She was also stringently opposed to divorce and believed that a woman's true place was beside her *man*. As equals, yes, but Dieulafoy believed that a woman's greatest worth was to be found not through independence but through partnership—found in a husband. The scholar Margot Irvine invites us to consider the scene in which Dieulafoy sharply reprimands a twenty-eight-year-old journalist who is bored by her husband, craving adventure, and considering leaving her marriage: "Divorce works against women, it annihilates them, it lowers their status, it takes away their prestige and their honor. I am the enemy of divorce."[26] She made the young woman cry, yet when she left the girl had "tears running down her cheeks but her face was beaming."[27] Dieulafoy offered a little more explanation, remarking, "I only wish to show that happiness comes from doing your duty towards others and not from satisfying your wishes and whims. The best way to love your husband is to love his soul, his intelligence and also the highest expression of himself, namely his work in the world."[28]

While some of the first women archaeologists found freedom roaming deserts and sailing away from the rules and rigmarole of Victorian society, Dieulafoy found freedom through marriage. It was as a wife that she released herself from consuming concern for her own wants and needs and latched onto something bigger. Through her version of selflessness, Jane found liberation. The young journalist "beaming" with tears in her eyes apparently saw the potential for the same.

As a couple the Dieulafoys were admired and teased. The manly Jane cut an eccentric profile, and jokes about "who wears the pants" in the Dieulafoy household were the stuff of comics galore. But they carried on unabashed about their boldly different marriage—or at least their *style* of marriage, in which man and woman both wore the pants. Both were famous in their own right: Marcel increasingly so as an archaeologist, and Jane not only as France's first popularly known woman archaeologist but also as a writer, photographer, essayist, and all-around literary figure. Their installations of Susa's artifacts and monuments at the Louvre brought them into the public spotlight, and crowds flocked to see the new Persian galleries.

Meanwhile, both Dieulafoys reaped rewards for their contributions to archaeology (and for bringing added prestige to France's museums); Dieulafoy was one of the very few women awarded a cross from the Legion of Honor. Between the two of them, distinctions between male and female were fluid, seamless, even elastic. They considered themselves a unified whole, and as Dieulafoy once began a speech, "When addressing the moon, one hesitates to use the masculine or the feminine form." Jane and Marcel were the Dieulafoy moon.

THE DIEULAFOYS' PASSION for Susa was stronger than ever, and they were anxious to return. Unfortunately, negotiations with the Persian authorities had come to a crawl. As troubles mounted and their return looked more and more difficult, Dieulafoy gave vent to her anger in a letter to the government in which she "dared to express her feelings regarding the political and social state of Persia and the way its sovereign ruled."²⁹ It was something no official wanted to hear, especially from the mouth of a woman. Some even suspect that the government withheld support precisely because of her gender. One scholar notes that another "one of the reasons the Dieulafoys weren't able to return to Susa was due to Jane Dieulafoy's involvement in the mission. It clearly went beyond what was expected of a dutiful wife at the time and other scholars were uncomfortable with her very active role."³⁰ In any event, the shah of Persia was offended. Dieulafoy had gone too far.

As Jane and Marcel waited for permission to continue their archaeological exploration of Susa, a man named Jacques de Morgan landed on the soil they loved so much. He traveled through the country from 1889 to 1891 and began to overshadow the Dieulafoys. Ultimately, he became director of the French Archaeological Delegation in Persia as the Dieulafoys sat wringing their hands in Paris. Susa became his. It was a stinging loss.

Persia was thus relegated to a dream and shared memories. As the years passed and they became further removed from the part of the world they loved best, Susa morphed into a phantom of inspiration. Dieulafoy wrote her first novel, *Parysatis*, with the ancient site as its backdrop. The book was filled with reconstructions of the ancient city—the palace walls and courts, monuments, and people were returned to vibrant life through her careful reconstructions of time and place. It later became a famous opera. Dieulafoy began to shine as a woman of literary stature and just as she had once seized the pickaxe in service of archaeology, she now took up the pen and made writing her cause. She fought alongside other prominent women authors of the day to open the gates of France's Académie and let the ladies in.

The work of highly regarded female authors was consistently denied recognition by French literary awards. In response, Dieulafoy and several other women, including Juliette Adam, Julia Daudet, Lucie Félix-Faure Goyau, Arvède Barine, and Pierre de Coulevain (many women writers used pseudonyms to publish at the time) came together in 1904 and helped to establish the Prix Femina. This new award helped to transform the face of French literature. The prize could go to either a man or a woman, but the jury was—and is to this day—exclusively female. Dieulafoy sat on the first jury. Even without Susa in reach, she was a celebrity in Paris.

Archaeology was still in the Dieulafoys' blood, however, and having lost Susa, the two set their sights elsewhere. Marcel's knack for archaeology revolved around making connections. Just as he had once sought the origin of medieval Western architecture in Asia, he now opened his research to include Spain and Portugal. The couple traveled extensively, much as they had on their first expedition through Persia, photographing the old buildings and churches.

Circumstances of war and serendipity also brought them to Morocco, where they hoped to actively excavate again and fuse their theories about how the Orient's architecture mingled with the West's. They embarked on excavations of a local mosque, and because Marcel was busy working for the engineering corps (part of what brought them there in the first place), Jane directed the work by herself.[31] Soon they were invited to excavate in other areas and were busy once again in the field.

All of that changed when Dieulafoy contracted amoebic dysentery through the unsanitary food and water on site. She was too weak to work, so the couple returned to France in hopes of renewing her health. She recovered quickly, and they rushed back to Morocco. But sickness struck again. Whatever strength she had regained back home withered away. She and Marcel left for France again and settled in their hometown of Toulouse, ready to see her heal for good. She made it through the following autumn and winter, but died in the spring. She was wrapped in Marcel's arms when she took her last breath at age sixty-five.[32]

A NEWSPAPER ARTICLE written when Dieulafoy was still alive reflected on the couple's marriage. Unlike other accounts, which poked fun at their unusual dress, this one celebrated it, noting in almost historic terms how "our time can showcase, for the generations to come, unique examples of great and beautiful households, like those of... the Dieulafoys. The wife becomes a collaborator with her husband, sharing the excitement of his work, his moments of enthusiasm and his moments of discouragement... What a beautiful sight, indeed."[33]

Most of the women chronicled in this book overcame odds and obstacles to succeed alone in a man's world. Dieulafoy shows us something different. The partnership between her and Marcel is a shift from feminist narratives that subtly (or stridently) exclude men from the trajectory of a woman's success. Dieulafoy was in lockstep with her husband, and he with her, and surely someone as trendsetting and smart as Dieulafoy could have achieved much in life with or without a man. Granted, her challenges would have been precipitously steeper if she had been solo, and gaining permission to excavate would have been nearly impossible. Nonetheless, the wives who excavated with their husbands were

ABOVE: Beloved companions Jane and Marcel Dieulafoy

collaborators in the truest sense, and Dieulafoy received more recognition than most.

In the history of women's contributions to archaeology, Dieulafoy took an important first step toward proving that a woman could not only accompany her husband to far-off places but could also ride alongside him on horseback for thousands of miles, oversee the workmen, contribute greatly to matters of scientific importance, and write about it all with flair. The writer who described their partnership as a "beautiful sight" was writing at a time when a woman was still viewed as a kind of asset to her husband, someone who could forward his career and enrich his place in the world. But change often comes in increments. Dieulafoy is a beautiful reminder that a wife is not destined to be a little lady in the kitchen, and was not so destined even in Victorian times. She can well be a boot-wearing, whip-carrying, brilliant mind who chooses her husband not to find comfort but to widen her world and even travel to its corners noted for being exceptionally *un*comfortable.[34]

To ask why Dieulafoy chose archaeology is to ask why she chose Marcel. The two choices are closely linked. Her relationship with him was the catalyst for adventure, and Dieulafoy was clever to recognize that through romantic love—as well as marriage to a man who did interesting things—she could open doors that would have otherwise remain locked (or at least very difficult to pick open). She certainly didn't *use* Marcel to get into the field; whatever intellectual pursuit he dedicated himself to would have been her adopted passion as well, the effort she selflessly supported, but Dieulafoy knew what she was after. She married a man she believed in. One that didn't conform to the common cut and who could help manifest her *own* dreams of important work and travel. For Dieulafoy, archaeology was something she loved as a part of, an extension of, Marcel. It stood alone as its own passion, but it was ignited by two minds that came together.

Dieulaofoy's legacy is often summed up in the thumbnail sketch of a curious woman who wore men's clothes. But a visit to the Louvre today, on a normal crowded day—digital cameras flashing, tourists in packs sweeping through the galleries like currents—finds the Lion Frieze of Susa still mounted. Tourists line up to see it. The colors of the enameled bricks, so carefully recorded by Dieulafoy, remain shiny and brilliant. Dieulafoy's own life story has the roar of a lion, and the ancient stones on display today, along with the multitude of Susa's smaller artifacts, are tokens of more than just an ancient city in Persia. They are mementos of the woman who lifted her pick with joy to uncover them, digging until her strength gave out.

ABOVE: Nuttall as a young woman, in traditional Mexican dress

ZELIA NUTTALL

· · · · ·

MEXICO'S

Archaeological Queen

"She was an archaeologist, and she had studied the Aztec remains for so long, that now some of the black-grey look of the lava rock, and some experience of the Aztec idols, with sharp nose and slightly prominent eyes and an expression of tomb-like mockery, had passed into her face."[1] These were the words of D.H. Lawrence in his novel *The Plumed Serpent*, describing a character named Mrs. Norris, who was based on hot-blooded yet refined Zelia Maria Magdalena Nuttall.

Lawrence continues, "She led the way in black little shawl and neat grey hair, going ahead like a Conquistador herself."[2] In her home, a Mexican estate of palatial proportions and colonial architecture, Nuttall—and in this case her literary doppelganger, Mrs. Norris—lived surrounded by dark pink bougainvillea and white roses, black obsidian knives, clay figurines, and painted potsherds. Here was a woman who "always put her visitors uncomfortably at their ease, as if they were captives and she the chieftainess who had captured them. She rather enjoyed it, heavily, archaeologically queening at the end of her table."[3]

D.H. Lawrence, like many important persons of the day, was a regular visitor to Nuttall's home, called Casa Alvarado, just outside of Mexico City in the town of Coyoacán. He stayed with her as his own fascination with Mexico took hold and he began to write romanticized and sexually charged works beneath the country's hot and "eternal sun." At Nuttall's house he immersed himself in her library of local mythology, history, and research. He ravaged her knowledge of Mexican culture, past and present, and it helped shape the backdrop to novels like *The Plumed Serpent*. In its pages, he presents Mexico as a dark place riddled with fear and evil, paganism, the relentless beating of sacrificial drums, speeding heartbeats, and phallicism. It's all rather intense, even over the top; the man delighted in exploring savagery in the face of civilization, and vice versa. For Lawrence, Mexico possessed a "great under-drift of squalor and heavy reptile-like evil." Whether or not Nuttall liked his work is uncertain, but Lawrence liked her. Nuttall won respect immediately, whether from scientists or artists, and as Lawrence put it, "The world is made up of a mass of people and a few individuals. Mrs. Norris [aka Nuttall] was one of the few individuals."[4]

Nuttall brought her own brand of fire, even sass, to her work. When people crossed her, they paid dearly. When people impressed her, they would find a kind and benevolent touch in her oversight. Above all else Nuttall was, as one scholar explained, "a *woman* anthropologist... the zest she brought to her studies and her squabbles with her colleagues are unmistakably feminine. One is reminded of a prima ballerina or first soprano." Whether or not femininity has anything to do with a propensity for "squabbles," Nuttall was attracted to controversy and could act the part of diva. The author goes on to note that it "is a mark of anthropology having come of age that a woman entering the field could be an esteemed scholar *and* remembered as attractive or exasperating as a woman."⁵

Attractive she was, not just in physique, but in mind and style. Nuttall was the archaeological queen who carried herself through Mexican libraries and landscapes with sincerity and grace. Exasperating because she was sure of herself, highly and at times hotly opinionated, full of wit and candor. She had a pinch of salt to her, a streak of chili heat. If she was challenged, and if she believed that challenge to be without merit, she had a knack for tearing a man down. Publicly and permanently. Nuttall did not appreciate being told she wasn't right about something because, well, she usually was.

ZELIA NUTTALL WAS born in San Francisco on September 6, 1857, just after the heyday of California's gold rush. It was almost a century before the Golden Gate Bridge would cross the bay, and the young city was characterized by rolling grass hills and sand dunes rather than the parks, piers, and skyscrapers of today. Zelia was the second of Dr. Robert Kennedy Nuttall and Magdalena Parrott's six children. The passion Nuttall would develop for Mexican archaeology was inherited from her Mexican-born mother, daughter of a wealthy San Francisco banker. When Nuttall was a little girl, Magdalena presented her with a copy of Lord Kingsborough's volume of *Antiquities of Mexico,* which contained lavish, hand-painted illustrations of Mesoamerican codices. While other children read fairy tales, Nuttall studied the exotic symbols painted in red and black inks, the strange creatures and pre-Columbian gods rendered in greens and black, headdresses topped by yellow feathers, ceramic pots lifted to the heavens and clearly filled with smoke, frothed chocolate (food of gods), and other rich imagery. One scholar notes that Kingsborough's work "immediately awakened her interest, and this interest developed into a life-long quest for information on Mexico, its archaeology and its early history."[6] If knowing what you want from life is truly half the battle, Nuttall was on destiny's path before the age of eight. She wanted the world of Mexican archaeology.

Nuttall's father was a native of Ireland who had arrived in San Francisco via Australia. He had a medical practice in California, but his own health was delicate, and, in hopes of improving it, they left the foggy coastline and moved to Europe. The Nuttall family traipsed around for the next eleven years, living in France, England, Germany, and Italy. Nuttall was educated along the way, becoming fluent in at least four languages and attending Bedford

ABOVE: View of San Francisco, 1847

College, a school exclusively for women, in London. When she and the family returned to San Francisco in 1876, Nuttall was nineteen years old and already had significant knowledge of the world. She was worldly. She was wealthy. She was also probably looking for a husband, one who could continue to provide her with a life of travel.

She met her match in a Frenchman named Alphonse Louis Pinart. An explorer, anthropologist, and linguist, Pinart spent his own fortune pursuing scholarly interests and participating in expeditions, most recently (at the time he and Zelia met) in the Pacific. During his career he traveled through the Aleutian Islands and Alaska and to the coast of South America collecting artifacts and "ethnological specimens." He also came to possess a legendary crystal skull that he bought off a shady French antiquarian named Eugène Boban.[7]

Pinart and Nuttall were married when the latter was twenty-three years old, and the two embarked on a honeymoon worthy of a pair of adventurous hearts: through the West Indies, France, and Spain. When they returned to San Francisco, Nuttall was pregnant and their daughter, Nadine, was born in 1882.

Despite their apparent compatibility, the relationship was an unhappy one. In 1884 they were formally separated. In the same year, Nuttall made her first trip to Mexico. She went for five months, accompanied by her mother, brother, sister, and baby girl. While she was there she began an intensive study of small terra-cotta heads she collected from the archaeological site of Teotihuacán. This was her first real archaeological undertaking, and the results were fruitful: in 1886 she published a paper in the *American Journal of Archaeology* and thereafter began to gain recognition as a bona fide scholar.

In 1888 Nuttall was finally granted her divorce from Pinart. She took full custody of their daughter and reclaimed her maiden name not just for herself but for Nadine too. From a lifetime of letters that Nuttall wrote to friends and colleagues, it's clear that her Nadine was *the* love of her life.

Zelia and Nadine Nuttall relocated to Dresden, Germany, and took trips to all the great European cities, where Nuttall buried herself in their museum archives for research. Her career took off with the speed of a blazing comet. In contrast to other female pioneers, whose success was acknowledged in fits and starts (or posthumously), Nuttall had star quality. Doors opened for her. Before she was thirty years old, Madame Nuttall had been appointed Special Assistant in Mexican Archaeology at the Peabody Museum of Archaeology and Ethnology at Harvard, a post she kept for the next forty-seven years. She was also elected to the American Association for the Advancement of Science. It's reasonable to say that Nuttall had become the original single-mother superstar.

IN DRESDEN, NUTTALL was working with the philanthropist Phoebe Hearst, mother of newspaper tycoon William Randolph Hearst and benefactor of the Museum of Anthropology at the University of California, Berkeley. Hearst provided scholarships to women students at the time and exerted her influence (and checkbook) wherever she could further worthy educational aims. Nuttall and Hearst were thus both women of means and far-reaching interests. They collaborated in gathering cultural artifacts from around the world to enhance Hearst's growing collection and material core for the museum she subsequently endowed. Hearst was the financier, Nuttall the huntress.

ABOVE: The Edison Electrical Tower at the Chicago World's Fair, 1893

In a letter dated September 21, 1896, Nuttall writes to Hearst from Morocco, describing herself in no uncertain terms as a "scientist." In addition, there is mention of her work in Russia, Egypt, and Switzerland. Yet a rare moment surfaces in her correspondence with Phoebe when she admits that "my undertaking was not an easy one—I felt the responsibility heavily at times and it was a great trial to be alone & so far removed from all counsel or help."[8] In spite of the hardship Nuttall faced (and, it seems, the loneliness), she played a critical role in amassing the thousands of ethnographic objects of the Hearst collection.[9] And if the task was not easy, she accomplished it admirably nonetheless.

It was also around this time that Nuttall became acquainted with Franz Boas, one of the most important figures in the history of anthropology. The two became friends at the 1893

World's Columbian Exposition in Chicago.[10] The fair opened on May 1, and Chicago's Midway was a kaleidoscope of outlandish exhibits, flashy architecture, food of every culinary persuasion (from pumpkin pie to escargot), and everything spectacular and strange, including the very first Ferris wheel. A 22,000-pound block of Canadian cheese vied for attention with an Egyptian cigarette booth. There were aquariums filled with exotic fish, giant California redwoods on display, a fountain of red wine, and a medieval knight sculpture made entirely of prunes. Side-shows and carnies called out to the crowds, and belly dancers shocked passersby with a risque "hootchy-kootchy" routine. Tambourines rang, train whistles clamored, volcano dioramas exploded and spat orange lava, and reconstructed "native villages" showcased cultures from around the globe. There was even a Moorish palace with funhouse mirrors and wax statues that was a sensation. New technological inventions like electricity were demonstrated to the crowd's excited *ooohs* and *ahhhhs,* and a walk through the Horticultural Building provided an explosion of color, a happy assault on the senses, a verdant paradise of flowers, and simulated environments that ranged from Mexican deserts to Japanese tea gardens.[11] Amid all this chaos and showmanship, Nuttall and Boas were huddled in "Department M," a section of the fair devoted to archaeology, physical anthropology (bones), ethnology, and history.

Nuttall was an exhibitor, and she presented a colorful spread of copied ornate codex pages, her own restoration of a Mexican calendar system, and paintings of Mexican feather shields. Boas was there as an arranger of the exhibits and as a collector.[12] Both presented papers at the International Congress of Anthropology, which took place at the fair. Even in a carnival atmosphere, serious business had its place.

The relationship between Boas and Nuttall, sparked that festive year in Chicago, can be charted through a lifetime of letters exchanged thereafter. Together they worked to recruit bright minds to the cause of anthropology, with special interest in training not just the boys at Ivy League schools but also the relatively disadvantaged and indigenous locals who had a stake in preserving their own heritage. One of Nuttall's later pet projects was to use all her connections and power to launch the training of a promising twenty-six-year-old man named Manuel Gamio from Mexico. She arranged for him to be funded and shipped abroad so that he could study with Boas at Columbia University in New York. Eventually Gamio returned to Mexico as the first well-trained archaeologist who could excavate scientifically and who would achieve lasting fame as the country's most famous archaeologist. None of it would have been possible without Nuttall's persistent work behind the scenes.

Perhaps most important, and what ties Nuttall, Boas, and Hearst together, was Nuttall's pivotal role in laying the foundations for the future of American anthropology on the west coast. Hearst had money to spend and wanted to construct a permanent home for all of her anthropological finds. The University of California also had a strong desire to establish a cutting-edge anthropology program on its campus. The state had such a diversity of indigenous culture, so much history, and so many archaeological sites, and there was mounting anxiety that it had not yet been examined.[13] California was the golden state, and it provided a golden opportunity for anthropology to apply its toolkit and figure out how indigenous cultures spread, change, and adapt over time. Willingly or not, the native population became the subject of fascination and research for a generation of new anthropologists and archaeologists.

Nuttall believed there was no one better qualified to lead the effort to set up a prestigious "centre of investigation" than Franz Boas. In a letter to Phoebe Hearst, dated May 19, 1901, Nuttall endorses her friend, saying, "I have the highest impression of Dr. Boas, who is high-minded, disinterested & devoted to the furtherance of scientific work." What she wrote about Boas was a reflection of herself: she too was fired up to yank anthropology up out of its lazy treasure-hunting habits and slap some shape onto it. Nuttall wanted process, great minds, modern science, and in the end, big and satisfying results. As she explained to Dr. Boas, "You can count on me for doing all I can to further the cause of our beloved science." [14]

NUTTALL NEVER FELL in love with a man, but she did fall in love with a house: Casa Alvarado. She had been planning to settle down in San Francisco, but upon meeting the handsome Mexican estate, soaked in historical charm, roses and sunlight, she dropped her plans, packed her bags, and moved to Mexico in November 1902.

The house had its own archaeological story. [15] Coyoacán is located along the contour edges of a lava bed that comprises the Valley of Mexico, home to twelve thousand years of human history. In Nuttall's backyard, remnants of ancient cultures could be found beneath orchard trees. One day Nuttall noticed children playing with small clay heads near her property. They looked so unusual that she paid the children for their toys and started looking for others. More pottery and ceramic figures surfaced, and there, in her very own garden, in collaboration with Gamio, she made the first study of Aztec pottery ever completed in a given site. [16] The archaeological queen thus lived atop her own Aztec ruins. Did dreams of old metal knives, grinning idols, potsherds, and stone utensils drift up from the ancient soil and into her bedroom at night?

By all accounts Casa Alvarado was unforgettably grand, and D.H. Lawrence describes its shape and mood as follows:

> The square, inner patio, dark, with sun lying on the heavy arches of one side, had pots of red and white flowers, but was ponderous, as if dead for centuries. A certain dead, heavy strength and beauty seemed there, unable to pass away, unable to liberate itself and decompose. There was a stone basin of clear but motionless water, and the heavy reddish-and-yellow arches went round the courtyard with warrior-like fatality; their bases in dark shadow. Dead, massive house of the Conquistadors, with a glimpse of tall-grown garden beyond, and further Aztec cypresses rising...[17]

The gardens were Nuttall's second passion, after archaeology. Even when planting seeds she sought to revive history. She collected and planted seeds from ancient Mexican plants that the U.S. Department of Agriculture had never seen before. Over each season, she cultivated the food of Mexican ancestors and grew indigenous medicinal herbs. A tribute to Nuttall notes that "her intense love of flowers and the long hours she worked over them made her an authority on Mexican gardens... A visiting archaeologist would as often find her training her roses as at work at her desk. She would continue her work and keep up at the same time a delightful talk on the newest "finds" in archaeology."[18] Nuttall's gardens were just one more way she connected to Mexican land, history, and culture.

Nuttall was also a tremendous host. Just about every archaeologist, traveler, artist, and person of note making their way through Mexico made a point of stopping in to see her. Some scholars were warmly encouraged to stay for extended periods of time. All were rewarded with stories from a woman who had her finger on the pulse of the city and its current politics, her mind wrapped around the country's ghosts and buried past. They also got tea and cookies.

There is one story of Nuttall's hosting aplomb, so curious, revealing, and persistent that it bears repeating. Two young male archaeologists stopped by the Casa Alvarado to pay their regards to Nuttall. Servants brought them into the house, and as they wandered the rooms, admiring the artifacts and furniture, Nuttall entered dressed elegantly in long skirts. She briskly walked across the hall to greet them, and as she walked her drawers inched southward until they slipped and fell down around her ankles. *Without breaking her stride,* she stepped straight out of them and shook the men's hands as if nothing unusual had happened at all. Meanwhile, her maid ran in, grabbed the knickers, and darted off. True or not, the story has been cited in a reputable source, and it does seem to reveal some essence or truth of Nuttall's personality: a lack of inhibition and an ability to glide through any misstep.[19]

Settled in Mexico, Nuttall became more involved in its archaeology than ever. She played a hand in setting up the International School of American Archaeology and Anthropology in Mexico City, and she was made Honorary Professor of Archaeology at the National Museum of Anthropology in Mexico. One of her more noteworthy discoveries was the Codex Zouche-Nuttall—folded screens made of animal skin or bark paper, covered with a thin coat of fine lime plaster and painted with bright colors in black outline—which she traced from the Monastery of San Marco in Florence, Italy, to the book's owner, Lord Zouche, who lived in England. This codex has been heralded as the "best-known and most thoroughly understood pre-Conquest Mexican manuscript in existence today."[20] Nuttall demonstrated that the codices were not simple "picture books," as had been assumed, but rather historical chronologies of great events. The scenes of marriage ceremonies, warriors, wild animals, childbirth, and sacrifice all told a lavish history of the land's early inhabitants.

Nuttall also stumbled upon the Drake manuscripts, records from the voyage of Sir Francis Drake and crew aboard the *Golden Hind* in the late sixteenth century. Working in the archives on one of her numerous research projects, Nuttall describes finding the "volume which chance literally threw across my path... It lay on the floor in a dark and dusty corner from which I carried it to the light."[21] The sea captain Drake was her girlhood hero, and she pored over the manuscript pages that detailed the strenuous ordeals he and his crew suffered. They were imprisoned and, while under watch, forced to give testimony about their motives for exploration. Nuttall was touched by the humanity of their voices and the intimacy of their words before their untimely deaths. She would "wonder that, after a lapse of centuries, their last utterances should have first reached me," bringing her to "sometimes feel as though, in some strange way messages from those men, long dead, had been entrusted to me for transmission to their living compatriots."[22] Nuttall always walked a line that was tethered between Mexico's past and present; history's ghosts wisely chose her to communicate any overlooked facts and to set the record straight.

For all of her life, ancient books and manuscripts were Nuttall's good friends. She could often be found in their company. Yet there came a day when the written clues and hidden histories she read pushed her out of the library, away from her desk, and into the field. She was fifty-three years old when it happened.

NUTTALL WROTE OF THE Island of Sacrificios, which is located off Veracruz: "a light house & 2 cocoanut palms are the sole landmarks on the islet which is but a half mile long."[23] It was a desolate strip of sand, covered with ruins and painted murals bleached by the sun. And it was bloody.

Like Amelia Edwards, who arrived in Cairo more by chance than design, Nuttall first explored the Island of Sacrificios because the steamer she was on for a pleasure trip had fallen victim to heavy northern winds. Stranded in Veracruz until the weather improved, she was pleased to plan an excursion to the island whose history she had read about for years. Nuttall and a small party of friends first set foot on the island on December 27, 1909; old potsherds were strewn on the beach like seashells. From an archaeological perspective, things looked very promising, and Nuttall returned two days later with a Mrs. Hamilton, a man named Señor Meneses, two engineers, and Mrs. Fortuño y Miramon. There were also two local men with the group, her indentured "peons," there to assist in the digging.

Before the workmen had unloaded their equipment, Nuttall was off by herself scanning the shore for vestiges of the island's past. She quickly detected a thick, imbedded layer of burnt lime, perhaps a place where it was originally manufactured. Carrying on, she spotted pieces of cement flooring and the base of a wall coated in plaster. She followed the base eastward until she was tracing a now-massive wall that ran east-west. Nuttall's excitement grew, and as she followed the foundations of an obvious archaeological site, she knelt to the ground and began to tear away soil and roots from the buried surface of a smooth wall. With immense pleasure she noticed that lines painted in red ocher curved along the face of the ancient structure. She put the team to work clearing the area, saving one job for herself: "I reserved for myself the delicate task of clearing the surface of the wall, perceiving as I did so that the red lines formed a fragmentary conventional representation of the feathered serpent, Quetzalcoatl."[24]

It was a great painted dragonish bird with a long history of Mesoamerican worship. Quetzalcoatl is tied to the island's ritual importance and its role as a place of human sacrifice. Nuttall was eager to reconcile chronicles from centuries ago with archaeological remains, and the appearance of Quetzalcoatl that first day must have seemed a good sign. The accounts she had pulled from forgotten archives describe the scene seafarers witnessed upon arrival at the island before 1510, including buildings that may have related to Nuttall's own unfolding discoveries:

> We found thereon some very large buildings made of mortar and sand ... There was another edifice made like a round tower, fifteen paces in diameter. On top of this there was a column like those of Castile, surmounted by an animal head resembling a lion, also made of marble. It had a hole in its head in which they [natives] put perfume, and its tongue was stretched out of its mouth. Near it there was a stone vase containing blood, which appeared to have been there for eight days. There were also two posts as high as a man, between which were stretched some cloths, embroidered in silk, which resembled the shawls worn by Moorish priests, and named 'almaizares.'
>
> On the other side there was an idol, with a feather in its head, whose face was upturned ... Behind the stretched cloths were the bodies of two Indians ... close to these bodies and the idol there were many skulls and bones.[25]

Perplexed, the ship's captain inquired about what had taken place there. Why were the two men dead? Records report that the following answer was given: "... it was done as a kind of sacrifice... that the victims were beheaded on the wide stone; that the blood was poured into the vase and that the heart was taken out of the breast and burnt and offered to the said idol. The fleshy parts of the arms and legs were cut off and eaten. This was done to enemies with whom they were at war."[26]

By 1572, the island had a reputation for being haunted by the "spirits of devils." And by 1823, another sea captain, an Englishman, noted that the "island is strewn with the bones of British subjects who perished in this unhealthy climate..." The Island of Sacrificios always lived up to its name, a destination of sacrifice, and even Nuttall would conclude, "It is strange how, during the course of centuries, the history of the island seems always to have been tragic and associated with some form or other of human suffering and death."[27]

In spite of the morbid past, Nuttall was excited about her project. She made plans to move into an "unattractive and uncomfortable" pair of rooms in an abandoned quarantine station on the island. For a woman in her early fifties, busy as a high-profile socialite, to forsake the comforts of a home she adored for life in the field, she must have been galvanized by the archaeological finds that could be hers. For here was material not bound in a book: it was real, and she could touch it and scrape away the sand to see what came up. Thrilled, she sent Boas a letter in 1910 outlining her plans for a "scientific mission." She also appealed to government for financial support and was assured that it would be forthcoming. She would receive a stipend of $250 toward her expenses.

Nuttall was delighted about her stroke of good fortune. She made plans to spend "some weeks" on the island and looked

ABOVE: Zelia Nuttall in her later years

forward to conducting a thorough exploration of the place, focusing especially on the mural she had uncovered and what appeared to be the temple described in sixteenth-century accounts.

As she made her travel arrangements, Nuttall was walloped by a series of blows. First, the government's Minister of Public Instruction decided to reduce her funding to only $100. It was an impossible amount, completely insufficient to meet her very modest needs. Second, her plan to explore the whole island was now severely compromised: she was told that she would have to confine her investigations to a small portion of the island. And third, the most unbearable, was that Nuttall would now be supervised. Because she was (just) a woman, she would require the oversight of a man: Salvador Batres, the son of an old archrival, Investigator Leopoldo Batres. Batres was notorious for smuggling artifacts from sites he was supposed to be protecting and selling them to foreigners. He also bungled the National Museum's entire classification system, deciding in his hubris that his predecessor's work was somehow insufficient (though by Nuttall's standards, it was quite good). Batres was widely regarded as an arrogant man and, in Nuttall's opinion, a lousy archaeologist. When the two came into contact, animosity flared.

The announcement read: "... he [Salvador Batres] should supervise her. This Office believes it to be indispensible that he should supervise everything relating to this exploration so that thus scientific interests of Mexico remain safeguarded..." Zelia must have choked with anger when she read this. Burning with indignation, Nuttall, the great expert on the island's history, had been reduced to a mere field assistant, a "peon." She wrote to Boas that "instead of being helped I was hindered in every way &

that conditions offered me were *impossible* to be accepted by any self respecting archaeologist."[28] Nuttall was incensed, and she resigned from her position as Honorary Professor at the National Museum to show it.

She wiped her hands of the whole affair, but it wasn't over yet. During Holy Week, Leopoldo Batres sneaked down to the island. A few weeks later the government newspaper published a formal notice that *Batres* had discovered the ruins on the Island of Sacrificios! Nuttall hit the roof. She quickly managed to have an article run in the *Mexican Herald* that drew harsh criticism of Batres's cocky behavior; she made a fool of him. Referring to this intellectual theft as "the only discouraging experience I have had in a long scientific career"[29] Nuttall began dishing out more shame to Batres, and she dished it out deep.

Her fingers alight with fury, Nuttall wrote a forty-two-page essay for the journal *American Anthropologist,* laying out her years of research, her expert knowledge of the island, her preliminary archaeological work, her theories, her field methods, and so on. The article is considered her most significant contribution to Mexican archaeology. Midway through, she breaks from her calm stream of methodical presentation of facts and finds to lambast Batres and his affiliates. She begins, "Knowing of the trying experiences that other archaeologists, foreign and Mexican, had undergone, I should have rigidly abstained, as heretofore, from having any dealings whatever with the Batres-Sierra coalition..."[30]

She had the attention of every anthropologist and archaeologist in North America reading the popular journal, and she used it to devastating effect. Not only did she ruin Batres's career, she humiliated the administration that had enabled him, noting with matter-of-fact coolness that it was no wonder this "coalition" had discouraged modern science and driven all true archaeological talent out of Mexico.

Just when the lynching seems complete, Nuttall sharpens her claws and rips into Batres again, this time criticizing his entire classification scheme for the museum's archaeology department with a string of embarrassing examples. Señor Batres was destroyed, finished. In contrast, Nuttall's reputation not only had been restored but was now brighter than ever. Everyone knew she was in the right. As a later obituary for her attested, "Mrs. Nuttall's vivid mind, independent will, and a remarkable belief in the truth of her theories caused her life to be punctuated with controversies." She was drawn to a good fight like a moth to light.

IN A DAY when there were hardly any women working in scientific fields, Zelia was regarded as "the very last of the great pioneers of Mexican archaeology."[31] She was one of the great pioneers to be sure, but most notably she was the only woman on a roster of men. She was prolific in her scholarly interests and pursued everything from the universalism of the swastika to archaic culture to ancient moon calendars. Over time some of her work has fallen into disuse—new material has proved old theories wrong, recent discoveries have revamped once trusty chronologies. Yet a large portion of her work is still relied upon today for its accuracy and erudition. It was Nuttall who decoded mysterious codices, who brought manuscripts to light, and who was able to unite disparate strands of research on Mexican artifacts and sites. Before she settled into life at Casa Alvarado she traveled extensively—collecting artifacts in Russia, navigating archives

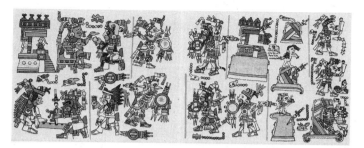

ABOVE: The Codex Zouche-Nuttall, one of Zelia Nuttall's most important discoveries

in Italian libraries—and even as a new bride, Nuttall lived the life of an anthropologist, debating questions of ethnology and ethics over breakfast.

What drew Nuttall to archaeology is a question that can be whittled down to an even finer point: what drew her to Mexican archaeology? For all her interest in world history, Nuttall's relationship with Mexico was deeply monogamous. Nuttall's path toward archaeology was illuminated when her mother handed her the picture books, when she first met the serpent Quetzalcoatl as an eight-year-old.

All of Nuttall's personal letters have been lost, and with them any personal expression of her passion for the field.[32] But one has only to look at her life: marriage, separation—Mexico (as if to seek inspiration at a difficult time); Europe, motherhood, a return to California roots and then a refusal, a seduction—Mexico again. Nuttall stayed in her beloved Mexico and Casa Alvarado until the day she died, in 1933 at age seventy-five. Her love affair with the country was best expressed through archaeology. It allowed her to engage with the past, present, and future of the land and culture she adored. She dug into its soil and found pieces of its heritage, she nurtured her native plants from volcanic soils littered with prehistoric ceramics to watch them bloom each spring, and she published her research and recommendations broadly to help inform preservation of Mexico's heritage for the future.

Nowhere is Nuttall's love for Mexico, past and future, clearer than in her article titled *The New Year of Tropical American Indigenes*, written toward the end of her life, in 1928. Through it, Nuttall seeks to restore indigenous Mexican culture to its living heirs. Aware of what was lost when the Spanish tore through and conquered the country, Nuttall was an early advocate for the revival of "Indian" traditions. She calls upon the poetics of the solar cult to breathe history's legacy into contemporary life with a traditional celebration of the indigenous New Year. She begins by explaining how in a region 20 degrees north and south of the Equator, "a curious solar phenomenon takes place on different days, according to the latitude, and at different intervals. In its annual circuit the sun reaches the zenith of each latitude twice a year, near noontime, and when this happens no shadows are cast by either people or things."[33]

This was the "beneficial descent" of the sun god to the earth. Nuttall goes on to detail how once "picturesque ceremonies" were held where "offerings consisting of gorgeous gifts made of precious stones, gold, silver, and other valuable minerals..." were laid at the foot of temples bathed in complete and shadowless sun twice a year. This ancient tradition was lost when the Spanish demanded eradication of the solar cult and ordered the sacred temples destroyed.

Nuttall hopes to restore this ritual of light and renewal to the people of Mexico. She voices her desire to see that "the children and young people not only of Mexico but of the other Hispano-American countries as well, bring back to life, as a school festival, the observance of the new year of their ancestors, placing in the grounds and gardens of their schools more or less simple gnomons, orienting the circles and lines of old." In Nuttall's opinion "it would be a charming as well as a patriotic and highly educational festival, the revival of such an ancient, such a typical, and such a purely Indian custom."[34]

Nuttall did not romanticize the past—her work at the Island of Sacrificios alone and its evidence of brutal human sacrifice would have made any attempt to present earlier days as idyllic seem silly. Her greatest strength as a researcher was in finding what the facts were. What the documents in lost archives revealed. What the strange language of codices hid within their stream of symbols and pictures. She was a scholar anchored more to modern science and method than to speculation or fancy.

For this reason, Nuttall's call to resurrect indigenous solar celebrations is sincere. She does not want to gaze at quaint Mexican culture from an ex-pat's balcony; rather, she summons the culture's own legacy. Nutall gave her heart to Mexico. And one gets the feeling that Mexico's ghosts were happy to have her there, fondly watching as she brushed away history's dust and dirt.

ABOVE: The extraordinary Gertude Bell, age fifty-three, 1921

GERTRUDE BELL

. . . . .

O, Desert Tiger!

"**S**he is only a woman, but Y'Allah she is a mighty and valiant one... If the women of the English are like her, the men must be like lions in strength and valor."[1] Such were the words of Bedouin sheik Fahad Bey, whom Gertrude Lowthian Bell encountered on her journey across the Arabian Desert in the winter of 1914. He may have wondered if all British women were like her, but the answer is certain: no other woman was.

A creature unto herself, Bell was an adventurer, intellect, archaeologist, photographer, author, diplomat and political strategist, poet, mountain climber, and ethnographer who deftly made her way through Bedouin camps, royal homes, and crowded Middle Eastern bazaars alone, save for the local men she hired as guides and muleteers. The most powerful and respected woman of the British Empire, Bell was a comrade of T.E. Lawrence (aka Lawrence of Arabia), adviser to Winston Churchill, the founder of what later became the Iraq National Museum, and author of the country's first antiquity preservation laws. Her life was a steady sequence of mighty accomplishments, her style ferociously smart.

Dubbed "Mesopotamia's Uncrowned Queen," "the Shaper of Nations," and "Daughter of the Desert," Bell inspires sweeping admiration. It's the Bell Spell. A tall and willowy redhead, galloping on horseback through the desert wearing a long fur coat, saddlebags bulging with money, photography equipment, books, and silk dressing gowns, she was legendary, and her life was the stuff of an epic tale. It was built of bravery, cleverness, love, and fight and punctuated by tremendous joys and tragedy. She was a headstrong woman "avid," her mother recounted, "of experience."

When her horse couldn't make it because the terrain was too treacherous, when her guides declined to hike to the top of a hill to find some rumored ruins because the incline was too steep, the intrepid Bell was off her saddle and trudging up that hillside on her own, dodging the thistle and baking under a blazing sun. In nearly everything she did, she exercised a clear determination to reach her goals despite the obstacles in front of her. Her physical and mental abilities were in synch: she was both famed mountain climber and honored Oxford scholar. With a body as agile as her brilliant mind, Bell was unstoppable.

But she was human too, imperfect and flawed, an impressive and indefatigable workaholic. On occasion she exhausted herself. Her work's legacy has fostered criticism and fueled foes. Her role in facilitating British colonialism comes under heat from scholars today, and she'll never escape her position as honorary secretary of the Women's Anti-Suffrage League in Britain.

Bell had a real taste for poetry both written and lived. Fluent in Arabic, Persian, French, German, and several other languages, she was a deep admirer of the Sufi poet Hafiz, and her early translation of his work is still considered one of the finest. Based on her books, letters, and diaries, we also find that Bell was a poet herself. As her stepmother remarked, "the spirit of poetry coloured all her prose descriptions, all the pictures that she herself saw and succeeded in making others see."[2] Her writing crackles with brilliance and wit, smolders with insight, both social and political. For such an accomplished woman there is also heartfelt emotion, at times vulnerability, in her writing. Take her description of a moonless night when she "scrambled over the heaps of ruin" and "...caught the eye of a great star that had climbed up above the broken line of the arcade, and we agreed together that it was better to journey over earth and sky than to sit upon a column all your days."[3]

Bell dreamed of travel and she journeyed far in a day when travel was arduous, maps were few, danger was daily, and the comforts of her English home were utterly absent. In agreement with the heavens, she lived daringly and uncompromisingly. And away from the routines of her affluent estate and family she took great pleasure when entertained by desert gossip, sitting at camp fireside, outside canvas tents, listening with rapt attention to stories of camel-lifting, blood feuds, and shifting tribal alliances.

As a scholar, Bell permitted her interest in archaeology—in visiting and recording the ruins, inscriptions, and mounds of the open deserts—to structure her incredible journeys. Her travels were frequently directed from one archaeological site to the next, each ancient building a touchstone of earthy purpose in her loftier pursuits of knowledge. Without her love of archaeology, Bell's explorations would have lacked a framework, almost as if she were traveling without destination. As she once noted, "The path of archaeology led me to the sheikh's door..."[4] Indeed, it was what led her everywhere.

GERTRUDE BELL WAS born to an upper-class family in England, the sixth-richest in the country, and the homes she lived in over the years were posh. Her father was Sir Hugh Bell, a well-to-do ironmaster and grandson to the powerful Isaac Lowthian Bell, one of the county's foremost and wealthiest industrialists. He was a mogul in the world of science and innovation. It was her grandfather's wealth that had made the Bell family rich, though her father carried on his own successful career.

The Bell family lived in a seaside house called Red Barns in the village of Redcar, near the town of Middlesbrough in North Yorkshire. This area was like an affluent suburb, conveniently close to, but far enough away from, the nearby industrial center of Middlesbrough, with its manufacture of iron and sooty skies. The family also owned a home in Belgrave in London, an upper-class neighborhood where political leaders and intellectuals of the day would get together in a regular ferment. The third home was Rounton Grange, also in Yorkshire, Bell's favorite. Built by her grandfather in the Arts and Crafts style, this house was where she did most of her writing.

Bell and her siblings grew up surrounded by lush English gardens, and each child always had his or her own little plot to tend. Bell's awareness of their seasonal production was keen. Notes she wrote as a little girl count off which types of flowers she found that day, how many, and where. The gardens of her youth gave Bell an eye for green, and in the deserts she later explored she would find and identify whatever had managed to photosynthesize. When she traveled, her letters home were flowery. Not in the sentimental sense, but in the botanical: fields carpeted by sheets of red anemones, breezes pungent with the fragrance of fig blossoms and Lebanon cedar. Her field notes bloom with wild almond and apricot trees, hills where "pale blue hyacinths lifted their clustered bells above the tufa blocks, irises and red anemones and a yellow hawkseed dotted the grass,"[5] and ruins where olive trees grew and vines rambled. Throughout her life, she took pleasure in spring wildflowers regardless of where she was. From picking countryside cowslips as a teenager with her sister Molly—"it is so heavenly here with all the things coming out and the grass growing long"—to decades later when she was sunburned, riding on horseback, and carrying a rifle to protect herself against desert soldiers, Bell always doted on a wilderness that "had blossomed like the rose." She catalogued plants as if they were all dear friends. "There was the yellow daisy, the sweet-scented mauve wild stock, a great splendid sort of dark purple onion, the white garlic and purple mallow, and higher up a tiny blue iris and red anemones and a dawning pink thing like a linum . . ."[6]

This love of botany was a connective element in Bell's life that joined two vastly different environments: Victorian England and the Middle East. Whether in a desert tent or canopy bed, the flowers she collected and kept by her bedside might well have been one of the most consistently and conventionally "feminine" things about her.

Her family consisted of her stepmother, Florence; her father, Hugh Bell; and their five children: Gertrude, Maurice (both step-children to Florence), Molly, Elsa, and Hugh, in descending order of age. They were close-knit, and what stands out most in the lifetime of letters Bell wrote home to them is an unshakeable familial affection. She never fails to express deep interest in every family event, from the selection of satin ribbons for party dresses to the marriages of her friends and sisters. Her letters home over a lifetime read like fast heartbeats in their constant excitement. In her early travels, they are filled with an enthusiasm for life that spills off the pages—as if every place and each new conversation were one of a kind, irreplaceable, almost too good to be true. Over and over again, she stuffed fast-written rapture into envelopes. Her letters would reach out to her family with open arms, in a rush of words: *To see you again would delight me so! I'd fall upon your neck.* Old-speak for a hug.

Bell was only four years old when her mother, Maria Shield, a delicate lady, died three weeks after giving birth to Bell's brother Maurice, in 1871. As a result of that loss, she developed a powerfully close relationship with her father, Sir Hugh Bell, which made them a bonded pair for life. From childhood through her adult years, Bell relied on her father for advice, opinion, support, and affection. At university, she would cite his opinions as authoritative, ending any of her heated arguments with a declaration of what Sir Hugh Bell thought on the matter. When she was a little girl, the two of them would stroll the countryside, ride horses, and chat by the fireplace. In later years, and as Bell's work became more complicated and more famous, and as the stakes grew ever higher, they corresponded regularly and she consulted him on matters political, financial, diplomatic, and strategic.

Sir Hugh visited his daughter abroad several times, and when she was without him, she missed him more than anyone. She reflected that "it is at times a very odd sensation to be out in the world quite by myself... I don't think I ever feel lonely, though the one person I often wish for is Papa." [7] Since Bell never married, the closeness she felt to her father only intensified over the years, never lessened or distracted by the attentions of a spouse.

After the death of his first wife, Maria, Bell's father married Florence Ollife, a sophisticated and well-connected twenty-four-year-old from Paris who had a strong influence on Bell's upbringing. She shaped her stepdaughter's manners—softening a natural impatience—her style of dress, and even her work ethic.

Florence wrote books of nursery rhymes and songs, plays, articles, and even an opera, and she devoted tireless effort to chronicling the lives of England's poor. Like Bell, Florence was industrious, intellectual, worldly. Yet unlike her mold-breaking stepdaughter, Florence was a more typical fit with her times. Women could conduct charity work for the common good of society, but that was extracurricular to family and home life. It was with real reluctance that she permitted her stepdaughter an education that exceeded piano lessons, homemaking, and hostessing. In her view, and in most peoples' then, too much education could be harmful to a young woman. Doctors even warned that too much thinking during a girl's teenage years could harm her reproductive abilities and her brain. Not to mention that too much skill in debate and world affairs might deter a suitor.

Still, Florence did some interesting and daring work herself. She interviewed destitute families and documented their experiences, using a kind of ethnographic approach to glean insights into hardships faced by England's poor. From this work came a massive book called *At the Works: A Study of a Manufacturing Town.* The conclusions she drew did little to remedy the situation or the cause of the problem—gut-wrenching poverty and a brutal class system—but the plight of lower-class families was described in sympathetic detail. By her work, she helped bridge understanding between one class and another and, more than anything else, stirred up some empathy. When her stepdaughter later crossed deserts and befriended the people that lived therein, she would employ a similar approach: sitting down with strangers to listen and learn.

As a young girl, Bell was powerfully smart. Feisty, hotly opinionated, boastful, and confident, Bell was always in pursuit of a verbal wrangling and a chance to broaden her own thinking. She devoured books. She demanded attention from the housemaids, loved to argue her point of view, and wanted to learn what people knew but was less inclined to feign interest in what they thought. Her interest in the common girlish lessons of sewing, music, and singing was minimal at best, but she was wickedly skilled at a riding a pony. She played sports, tortured her brother with dares, and threw her dog in the lake just . . . because.

Her governesses and teachers were exasperated by Bell and astonished by her quick mind and aptitude for learning. As her intelligence became increasingly apparent, the teenage Bell became more and more impervious to the monotony of her at-home schooling and restless with the insatiable drive that eventually came to define her. She was also argumentative and bossy, and her parents recognized that the normal sequence of events for a girl Bell's age—the formal introduction to society, a time to court and spark, a wedding and children soon after—wasn't going to fly. When she was fifteen they made the exceptional decision to send her to Queen's College, an all-girls' school in London. From there, Bell's razor-sharp intellect and her professors' persuasive recommendations that she continue her education allowed her to carry on her studies at Oxford in 1886. Once enrolled, she started attending the Oxford Archaeological Society meetings.

Bell was at Lady Margaret Hall, one of the two women's colleges at Oxford, and while living on campus she was, as one of her biographers put it, "something of a social hand grenade."[8] No doubt she was frustrated by the restrictions placed on her because she was a woman: always required to have a chaperone to go anywhere, treated as an unwanted interloper in an almost exclusively male environment, often made to sit at the back of the room and told to hush. But she aired her thoughts freely and without a second's hesitation and even told off her male teachers when she felt they deserved it. To her female counterparts, she was a hero. Her friend and fellow student Janet Hogwarth would later write in memory: "Gertrude Lowthian Bell, the most brilliant student we ever had at Lady Margaret Hall...—alive at every point, the vivid, rather untidy, auburn-haired girl of seventeen... took our hearts by storm with her brilliant talk and her youthful confidence in her self and her belongings."[9]

By the time Bell completed her studies at Oxford, in a remarkable two years instead of the normal three, she was the only woman to have ever taken a First in Modern History. This was (and remains) the greatest academic achievement that could be awarded a student, male or female. Although her degree was never formally awarded—Oxford did not extend hard-earned degrees to female students until 1920—Bell's own glee about her monumental accomplishment shines in a quick letter to her stepmother. Dated 1889 in London, it read: "Minnie Hope was sitting with an Oxford man. Presently he grabbed her hand and said 'do you see that young lady in a blue jacket?' 'yes' said Minnie lying low. 'Well,' said he in an awestruck voice, 'she took a first in history!!'"[10] She did, and soon afterward she was off to begin a series of journeys across uncharted, archaeologically rich lands that would eventually make her a significant figure *in* history herself.

THE EXTENSIVE TRAVELS that Bell would embark upon were possible not only because she had gumption but also because her family had money and influence. Florence's relations and friends abroad allowed Bell to start a traveling career as the doors of all the French and British embassies were flung open wide in welcome.

It was in 1892, at the age of twenty-four, that she got her first taste of the Middle East. Persia, the place she had "always longed to see," was to be hers for six months. Florence's sister Mary and her husband, British Ambassador Frank Lascelles, had invited Bell to join them on a tour. In preparation, Bell tackled Farsi and achieved basic fluency. Mastering multiple languages became a trait of hers. She spoke French, German, Persian, Arabic, and enough Hindustani and Japanese to get by. Although she had an exceptional talent for learning languages, she still struggled when she started. Practicing Arabic, she complained to her father in a letter: "I thought I should never be able to put two words together... there are at least three sounds almost impossible to the European throat. The worst I think is a very much aspirated H. I can only say it by holding down my tongue with one finger, but then you can't carry on a conversation with your finger down your throat can you?"[11]

In Persia, Bell stayed in Teheran, where she fell in love with scenes of stone and sand. The desert's vastness thrilled her; she thought its miles of nothingness were wonderful. She must have seen something of herself in its stretch, aware that the desert was uniquely suited to absorb her boundless energy. She continued to travel around the world with her father or her brother Maurice for the next seven years, and it wasn't until 1899 that she returned to the Middle East. Then she began to hear the siren's song of archaeology and made it her lifelong passion.

BELL'S WORK AS an archaeologist was more dangerous and more bug-ridden, unmapped, and exposed to harsh conditions and hazards than that conducted by any other woman before World War I—and, safe to say, by most men too.[12] She normally traveled on horseback, occasionally by camel, and always alone except for the men she hired. It was often so scorching hot in the deserts that she wore full-length coats to ward off the white

ABOVE: One of Gertrude Bell's field tents

sun's rays: "The sun was so hot it burnt one through one's boots. I have gone into linen and khaki. The latter consists of a man's ready-made coat, so big that there is room in it for every wind that blows, and most comfy; great deep pockets. The shopkeeper was very anxious that I should buy the trousers too but I haven't come to that yet."[13] Unlike Jane Dieulafoy, Bell never wore pants. She refused. Although she was sometimes mistaken for a man or boy, greeted as *Effendim!* (my lord) by desert Druze and Bedouin men, once she spoke, unwrapped the veils from her face, and took off her coat, there was nothing manly about her.

Bell was a fashionista. Her wardrobe was all dressing gowns, velvet wraps, feathered felt hats, and crêpe de chine blouses. Her travel bags held porcelain china to dine on and crystal, delicate as her own English features, to drink from. Bell understood her power as a European woman abroad, and she never apologized for being a lady. She basked in her own sense of rarity and strode through even the most extreme field conditions in a skirt.

But she was practical too. In her post-Oxford, pre-archaeologist days Bell passed the time with a little mountaineering (she was a real hobby conqueror). She scaled icy ridges and high peaks in the Swiss Alps numerous times, had a particularly ferocious mountain named after her thanks to the glory of her ascent of it, and went down in the pages of climbing history as the unparalleled "prominent lady mountaineer" of her time, one who was venerated by the following praise: "of all the amateurs, men or women ... [there were] very few to surpass her in technical skill and none to equal her in coolness, bravery and judgment."[14] In her coolness, she took off her cumbersome skirts while climbing and made her way up rocky overhangs in only her undergarments. Clothing, though adored by Bell, could be left behind as easily as pretense and convention when circumstances required.

But there's no doubt she loved her pretty things. She always perused the Harrod's catalog to keep up with trends, and as a young woman in 1899 she would write to her sister Elsa, "My new clothes are very dreamy. You will scream with delight when you see me in them!" Much later, as a woman of fifty, masterminding and maneuvering in high political circles, she would still write her stepmother to ask for the latest styles in fashion—for a silk evening dress to be shipped her way by post, for "a green silk woven jacket thing with silver buttons," please. She used both her elegance and the polished manners she inherited from her stepmother to advantage.

Pearls and feathers aside, Bell was still resilient in an unfriendly field. Despite the luxuries she grew up with, she could happily forsake lamb suppers, cream scones, and tea for big bowls of milk, sour bread, and *dibbis* (a sweet date syrup) and, on special occasions, sheep. She didn't flinch from drinking muddy water—only declining a sip from cisterns that were "full of little red animals swimming cheerfully about." Most mornings she breakfasted on "dates, camels' milk and the bitter black coffee of the Arabs—a peerless drink." For a treat there was white coffee: hot water, sweetened and flavored with almonds. On some hard nights when starry darkness settled in on what Bell called "starvation camp": only rice and bread to nibble and no charcoal for fire or barley for the horses. [15]

Outfitted in her long coat, she would withstand days of travel, some ten or more hours long, after which she would feel "as if I had been sitting in my saddle for a lifetime and my horse felt so too." Her face was whipped by blowing sand, rain, sun, snow, and ice and sometimes clouded in warm, eerie mists that made the landscape around her disappear. The terrain ranged from sloping dunes to a crumbling rock that made the horses slip and skid, to yellow mud the "consistency of butter" [16] that threatened to swallow her team whole, pet dog included.

Come bedtime she endured a variety of makeshift camps. Some were pleasantly tucked into flowered hillsides, quaint villages close, running streams nearby; others were thick with black beetles or rocky affairs where a mattress was mere thistles and her bed fellows stinging flies. Most of her experiences seem to have kept her in high spirits, though, and were preferable to some stifling social event with English ladies. As she put it, "This sort of life grows upon one. The tedious things become less tedious and the amusing more amusing..."

Bell received an allowance from her father that financed each of her excursions. Although she was in charge of most aspects of her life, she never held her own purse strings. Without Hugh Bell's support, Gertrude Bell's legacy would never have been

ABOVE: Bell picnicking with Iraq's King Faisal and company, 1922

realized. His support, permission, and financing is what allowed her to travel. Today a young woman can travel independently and on the cheap—by teaching English abroad, working as an au pair, backpacking, being an exchange student—but in the late nineteenth and early twentieth centuries, to travel at all was pure luxury. Even if that luxury included bug-infested tents, fevers, and meals of sour milk, the whole lot required a sizable investment. Horses had to be purchased, guides hired, cooks and servants employed, sheiks paid with handsome gifts, officials bribed, villages wooed, postage on a thousand letters home paid, and all the equipment a rigorous desert journey required—from pistols to bedding—purchased and packed. The Dieulafoys had a similar shopping list.

All this effort was driven by archaeology. Bell was passionate about it. A visit to Petra in 1900 introduced her to the grandeur of history. Located in Jordan, the "rose-red city half as old as time" was carved entirely out stone. Its beauty caught hold of her:

...we rode on and soon got into the entrance of the defile which leads to Petra ... oleanders grew along the stream and here and there a sheaf of ivy hung down over the red rock. We went on in ecstasies until suddenly between the narrow opening of the rocks, we saw the most beautiful sight I have ever seen. Imagine a temple cut out of the solid rock, the charming facade supported on great Corinthian columns standing clear, soaring upwards to the very top of the cliff in the most exquisite proportions and carved with groups of figures almost as fresh as when the chisel left them, all this in the rose red rock, with the sun just touching it and making it look almost transparent ... It is like a fairy tale city, all pink and wonderful.[17]

This was the city of later Indiana Jones fame (the backdrop to *Indiana Jones and the Last Crusade*), and today Petra is a popular tourist destination and designated UNESCO World Heritage Site. But in Bell's day it was empty—quiet and, for those who ventured so far to see it, all theirs to enjoy. After falling in love with Petra, Bell always "wished to look upon the ruins." Between 1905 and 1914 her work and desert travel were structured, even dominated, by archaeological study. She carefully recorded the ancient sites and remnants of buildings scattered throughout the Middle East, and she was often the first European, man or woman, to see an ancient site and to announce its existence to scholars back home. In archaeology, all her talents found a unique point of intersection. Her study of history at Oxford, all the languages she spoke (including myriad dialects of Arabic), and her high taste for adventure all merged into a single, passionate pursuit. For the rest of her life, archaeology would remain her biggest joy. As she once said, "I always feel most well when I am doing archaeology."[18]

ABOVE: Unlike Jane Dieulafoy, Bell never preferred to wear trousers in the field

AMELIA EDWARDS TOOK a life-changing trip, the Dieulafoys tackled the world together, and Zelia Nuttall eventually settled in her favorite place, becoming deeply enmeshed in its culture and history. Gertrude Bell simply rode and rode and rode. Bell's life was more about the journey than about getting there, and she grew to be as nomadic as the Bedouins who shared fire and food with her.

The maps Bell made as she traveled uncharted deserts became lifelines for those who would later follow in her footsteps. In addition, she had two great and lasting credits: the first was her work in the field, and the second her role in establishing the Iraq National Museum in Baghdad, where she also wrote the country's first antiquity laws.

Bell carried an early Kodak camera on her travels and took nearly seven thousand photographs between 1900 and 1918. Most of them feature archaeological ruins and desert tribes.[19] To this day, these black and white images are consulted for their accuracy and rare glimpse into a time untouched by Western influence. As a field archaeologist, Bell's most significant contribution was this incredible visual record of archaeological sites, inscriptions, cultural landscapes, and sundry features of architectural and artistic value.

She never participated in a true season of excavation, partly because of her love of independence and partly because she was never invited to join a team. Single women were simply not included in respectable field crews in the Middle East at that time. Nevertheless, no one could deny her knowledge of archaeology, and she also helped to finance some projects, earning her a bit of an "in." It is most accurate to say that Bell focused her efforts on archaeological *expeditions*—visits to survey, map, and record

ABOVE: Bell's field tent pitched in the shadow of ancient ruins

sites—rather than archaeological *excavations*, where she would have unpacked and stayed put to dig in.

In 1905, at the age of thirty-seven, Bell romped through Syria in a state of bliss, visiting with the Druze people and writing of her adventures in *The Desert and the Sown*, a book so well loved that it is still in print today. Like Bell's own field journeys, this book invited the reader to gaze upon those ruins with her, illustrated as it is with scattered photographs of statues and sphinxes, ornate column fragments, and pots. The same year *The Desert and the Sown* was published, 1907, Bell also authored a series of important articles in the journal *Revue Archéologique* about her findings during an excursion from northern Syria through Turkey, where she examined early Byzantine architecture. She was becoming increasingly prolific in her archaeological writing.

In the field, Bell's greatest distinction came from her work at a site called Binbir Kilise in south-central Turkey. Her archaeological investigations at this site and surrounding areas included "churches, chapels, monasteries, mausoleums, and fortresses that had never been previously described or mapped."[20] She collaborated with William Ramsay on this project, and in 1909 they published a book on their findings called *The Thousand and One Churches*. Although Bell had contributed 460 pages and Ramsay 80, the book still listed Ramsay as the primary author.

Bell's love of archaeology took her to Greece, Paris, Rome, and beyond, as well as through the deserts of the Orient and eventually to Mesopotamia, the future home of Iraq. Through it all she was attuned to the archaeological essence of the landscape, to its potential for containing lost histories, and was distressed when corn was planted on tells because the harvested roots might disturb the stratigraphy. She was also becoming ever more attuned to archaeological nuance. A scattering of stones that might represent an old wall, a shift in soil color that might signify disturbance to an area, a hill-like mound that might contain a buried fortress—Bell was on the lookout. Her appetite for archaeological discovery was never sated. Even at dinner parties her archaeological prowess would spill forth like the amply poured wine. She would speak of this or that new site, a fresh argument made in an excavation report, or delight in new theories explaining how the first people crossed over to North America via the Bering Strait leaving a trail of stone tools and bison bones behind them.

In 1917 she arrived in Baghdad, and it was here that her life took a new course, culminating in a line of work she found vital, essential, absolutely critical: the creation of an autonomous Arab state. Her knowledge of Arabic language, desert tribes, factions, leaders, and geography was of strategic importance to the

British military, and she was invited to work in Baghdad for the Arab Bureau—the only woman in a cabinet of men. The High Commissioner of Iraq, Sir Percy Cox, appointed her Oriental Secretary.

In Baghdad it was so hot that "the days melt[ed] like snow in the sun." She bought her first house, filled it with potted jasmine and mimosa, with woven carpets and pet dogs, and got comfortable, but she soon began to run bad fevers and write letters home in which she tried her cheerful best to shrug off any concern for her latest cold or flu. Outdoor temperatures reached 120 degrees Fahrenheit every day, cooling only slightly just before dawn broke. She went from lean to thin, from inexhaustible in the saddle to fatigued at her desk, and though she clearly found her work in Baghdad thrilling and momentously important, the gaiety of her field days was replaced by a slightly stressed tone. Vita Sackville-West visited Bell in 1926 and wrote:

> I had known her first in Constantinople, where she had arrived straight out of the desert, with all the evening dresses and cutlery and napery that she insisted on taking with her on her wanderings; and then in England; but here she was in her right place, in Iraq . . .
>
> She had the gift of making everyone feel suddenly eager; of making you feel that life was full and rich and exciting. I found myself laughing for the first time in ten days . . . [She was] pouring out information: the state of Iraq, the excavations at Ur, the need for a decent museum, what new books had come out? what was happening in England? The doctors had told her she ought not to go through another summer in Bagdad, but what should she do in England, eating

out her heart for Iraq?... but I couldn't say she looked ill, could I? I could, and did. She laughed and brushed that aside.[21]

It was an apt portrait of the nonstop Bell, hugely busy with work, engaged, chatty, and curious. At the time of Sackville-West's visit, Bell was involved in strategic decision making to lay the foundations for a new nation and its government, and her work was fueled not only by a rarefied understanding of Arab culture but by a genuine appreciation of that culture and its people. In keeping with the prevailing views of the day, however, Bell was an advocate of indirect British rule, and she subscribed to the tenets of colonialism, viewing the world through an imperial lens, a world perceived to be in need of Britain's civilizing assistance when in fact it wasn't. She was a product of her time, and just as she could refer to the people of Jabal el-Druze as great friends, she could simultaneously liken the Arab population to an "unruly child" in need of obedience training.

She worked tirelessly to see that Amir Faisal was installed as king of Iraq, and in 1921 he was. While in tenure, Bell wrote strategic reports and white papers so clever that people questioned whether a woman could really have done it. In a letter to her father she explained that "the general line taken by the Press seems to be that it's most remarkable that a dog should be able to stand up on its hind legs at all—i.e., a female write a white paper. I hope they'll drop that source of wonder and pay attention to the report itself..."[22]

During her time in Iraq, Bell founded the Iraq National Museum and was appointed Director of Antiquities and Chief Curator. In the latter role, her abilities matured from choosing to exhibit certain artifacts "wildly according to prettiness" to selecting materials based more on their archaeological and scholarly value.[23] Her commitment to Iraqi archaeology was firm, and with the power given to her as well as her own initiative, she collected, catalogued, and installed a vital collection for the new museum she loved and referred to fondly as her own. In the early 1920s she also helped to orchestrate major archaeological excavations at several Iraqi sites. British and American universities conducted these investigations, and their findings bolstered the prestige of the museum where "such wonderful things are to be seen." Scholarly recognition of Iraq, ancient Mesopotamia, increased, and the very cradle of human civilization was now seen as the source of some serious archaeology.

For all of her archaeological accomplishments, both in the field and in the museum, it was her visionary idea for the Law of Antiquities that set the greatest precedent and served not just the new Iraqi government but archaeology in general. Like Amelia Edwards, Bell was disturbed by the loss and destruction of archaeological treasures. Enacted in 1924, this law prohibited digging up archaeological sites on private land or anywhere else without an authorized permit. In short, it put an end to unchecked looting and plundering. It also stipulated that the results from an excavation be published so that all scholars would benefit from the discoveries and subsequent advances in understanding the region's history could be made.

The law was a progressive one, and it met Bell's own needs as Museum Director of Antiquities and Chief Curator too: archaeologists from overseas could no longer dig a site and take the prized artifacts back home with them. The gold would stay put, as would the best of the sculptures and friezes. The best finds would be installed at the museum. It was one of the first promises to a country that it would have the right to preserve its own heritage, within its own borders and for its own people. Bell had provided the people of Iraq with a protective measure to legally safeguard their history from greed and future threats.[24] As the archaeologist Max Mallowan (husband of Agatha Christie) noted, "No tigress could have safeguarded Iraq's rights better."[25]

THERE IS ANOTHER element to Bell's love of archaeology, a personal one. Archaeology allowed her to pack her bags, to fill her mind, and to focus her love on something that could never disappoint her or be taken from her. She chose archaeology as a way of life because it was reliable (there would always be more to find buried beneath the ground) and endlessly surprising (one never knew what would be found). She was skittish about loving objects not built of stone, for she had fallen in love twice and had her heart broken each time. Thus, some have ascribed Bell's insatiable travel to an unparked heart.

She met Henry Cadogan early in her travels to Persia. He was a young, bright scholar and could ride a horse as well as she. The two would read Sufi poetry and tear through the Persian deserts at a fast gallop, laughing to the wind, exhilarated. When Henry proposed, Bell accepted happily. Her parents, however, did not receive the news happily. Henry was a rumored gambler and did not have the kind of money and financial stability the Bells thought necessary for their daughter. Hugh Bell forbade the union, and Bell accepted the news with a heavy heart. She returned to England as her parents demanded, and not long afterwards Henry Cadogan fell off his horse into a frozen river and died of pneumonia.

When she fell in love again, it was twenty years later. Dick Doughty-Wylie could match her worldly accomplishments and excited her in both body and mind. A military man, Dick was dutifully, if unhappily, married to a "little wife" named Judith. Bell didn't hold her in very high esteem. In general, she found most English wives boring and once quipped, "The devil take all inane women."[26] Yet Bell was a steadfast believer in marriage and upright behavior and had no intention of adultery; she simply fell deeper and deeper in love with Dick over several years and through the pages of his correspondence, all of which she knew by heart.

From the letters they exchanged, it is clear that the fondness was mutual. Bell would find ways to see him alone, sending invitations to the Doughty-Wylie couple when she knew Judith would be away, and even if her family detected flirtatious, slightly improper behavior, Bell was now forty-four years old and they left her to it. She declined an invitation to travel through the Karakoram Mountains in China on expedition so that she could stay in England, where the parties, days of hunting and sporting, and other social events kept her close to the man she wanted to marry.[27] For Bell to decline adventure, the desire to stay near her beloved must have been bone-deep.

Yet Dick was not prepared to leave his wife or put his career and reputation at risk. Although he and Bell had one private encounter while he was paying an extended visit to the family home Rounton Grange—the door closed, the house asleep—Bell declined the intimate advance and remained a virgin her whole life.[28] Dick subsequently shied away from the intensity of the relationship and began to cool. His letters grew increasingly stiff and formal, and he eventually announced that he and his wife were moving to Albania.

Devastated, Bell began devising her own (even bigger) adventure back to the Middle East to soften the jilting blow and to keep her chin up. In response to news of her travel plans, Dick wrote in a letter: "Have a good journey—find castles—keep well—and remain my friend." Was he being trite? Find castles? *Friend?* She would find some castles to be sure. She threw herself into a desert journey that was almost painful—so demanding and so long that it's hard to know if she was hoping the trip would be a salve or so exhausting that it would numb whatever feelings she wanted gone.

The two corresponded for years, and sparks of warmth and passion would continue to flash now and then. They kept Bell's heart hopeful. Then, at a luncheon in London, Bell overheard a stranger comment on how unfortunate it was that Dick Doughty-Wylie had recently died in battle. Such a cavalier way to hear such crushing news. It was a killing blow.

In spite of Bell's life adventures and achievements, she wanted marriage and family life very much. She would be midwife to modern Iraq but would never be a mother. If thwarted love wasn't the very reason Bell traveled as hard and as far as she did, it is certainly what she thought about as she rode her horse for hours alone in sandy silence.

"ARE WE THE same people I wonder when all our surroundings, associations, and acquaintances are changed?" Bell asked in a letter home.[29] Was she? Was the multitalented, ever-busy Bell the same person through it all? Beyond the laurels and accolades, who was this person? It's a question that underlies much of Bell's story: her own quest for personal definition. Despite all her accomplishments and contributions, Bell seemed to be after a deeper understanding of herself and her claim on happiness. As she hurled herself at whatever challenges were presented to her, one suspects that in her tireless exertion what she really sought to discover was her own peace and calm.

In distancing herself from the constraints of Victorian society, Bell embarked on a series of adventures that allowed her to suspend, at least temporarily, her gender. When she dismounted from her horse at the end of a journey, when she was little more than a darkened silhouette against a twilight sky, she transcended categories of masculine or feminine and existed simply as a strong spirit uncommitted to other people's ideas of how things should be. Travel was liberation. And as she wrote in the opening page to *The Desert and The Sown*, "To those bred under an elaborate social order few such moments of exhilaration can come as that which stands at the thresholds of wild travel."[30]

Bell epitomized a woman's worth through her life of action and intellect even if she typically did so in isolation from other women (physically, emotionally, intellectually). She *was* anti-suffrage. While countless women took to the streets to march, struggling and protesting for their equal rights, Bell fought against that. The Honorary Secretary of the Anti-Suffrage League, she believed that women were not yet prepared to make decisions in the matters of government and state. They were too consumed by house and home, Bell believed, and until they collectively decided that their interests did and should rest beyond the home, they were unprepared to make decisions about how a nation should be governed. So while she was a crusader in showing the world what a woman is capable of, she did it alone (as she liked to do most things) and never championed other women. We can wish she was a great-grandmother of feminism, but she wasn't. She was a female maverick who thrived in a man's world. In turn, she thought as most men did and considered a lot of ladies to be dull as dogs.

By the time she was in her late fifties, Bell's obligations in Baghdad had been fulfilled and her next role was uncertain. Her family's financial resources had become strained, and although her work in Baghdad had lost its urgency after King Faisal was installed, she had little desire to leave Iraq and return to a life in England. Suddenly exhausted by a life lived with such forward-moving gusto, weakened by the Baghdad summers, and frightened that she might experience the unbearable loss of her father, the larger-than-life Bell began to quiet down.

She wrote a note to a friend in Baghdad asking him to look after her dog should "anything happen to her."[31] The next morning the unstoppable Gertrude Bell was found still. She had died in the night, an empty bottle of sleeping pills on her bedside table. Whether her death was an accident or suicide isn't certain, though circumstances suggest the latter. It was July 1926, and she was just a few days shy of her fifty-eighth birthday. One of her many obituaries summed it up: "At last her body . . . was broken by the energy of her soul."[32]

She was buried in a small cemetery in Baghdad, her bones laid to rest in the landscape she felt best in—the desert. Baghdad mourned her, Britain grieved, and those who knew her best were hollowed. What fortune she had left was bequeathed to the Iraq Museum.

ABOVE: Harriet Boyd Hawes sorting potsherds at her desk

HARRIET BOYD HAWES

. . . . .

JUST LIKE A

Volcano

*I*n her book *Born to Rebel: The Life of Harriet Boyd Hawes,* the author, Boyd Hawes's daughter, Mary, recalls a strange scene. They were traveling together on a small cruise ship and had arrived at the island of Santorini in Greece. Her famous mother still asleep, Mary walked onto the boat's deck to find that the engines had been turned off and that the world had been unexpectedly transformed into a "wonderland." They were afloat "inside the crater of a vast volcano." From within, "its huge black and coloured walls rose straight up, in places a thousand feet, from the bluest waters... Every eight or ten minutes great clouds of smoke or vapour coiled upwards from the cone, called the New Furnace; and a rumble or roar would break from the volcano." [1] The year was 1926, Harriet was fifty-five years old (her daughter sixteen), and it seemed perfectly apt that the woman who lived her life with explosive power should casually journey into the heart of an active volcano. Afterwards, mother and daughter scaled the sheer sides of the rock face and zigzagged to the top on donkeyback, just to see a beautiful old monastery and its ruins.

To compare Harriet Boyd Hawes to a volcano is no overstatement. Her tiny frame of just over five feet packed the power of a giant, and she exerted a decisive and active will always bent on achieving the things she believed in. Her life's work included Greek archaeology—and lots of it—as well as nursing for the Red Cross in the direst of war conditions, teaching, lecturing, and being a wife and a mother. She also had a tireless commitment to politics and justice that brought her into private conversations with illustrious figures such as Queen Olga of Greece and First Lady Eleanor Roosevelt. Deliberately seeking Boyd Hawes out, the U.S. president's wife took her by the hand and said, "I want so much to hear what you have to say." [2] Everyone did, and even if they didn't, Boyd Hawes typically made herself heard anyway. She was, as her daughter described, "super-charged."

She was also an American, one of the few female archaeologists of the period who didn't come from European soil. That didn't mean she wouldn't make her way across the Atlantic, though. Undecided about what to pursue in life, Boyd Hawes was traveling through Europe on a "grand tour" in 1896 in the company of other young women and under vigilant chaperone. She knew she wanted advanced learning in either history or the classics, which she loved, and she was pondering over where to study when an acquaintance asked, "Why go to England and study Homer and Plato under dull, grey skies, when Greece is there to teach you more than you can ever learn in books?" [3]

It seems that was all she needed. Turning her back on the ivy-walled libraries of her East Coast youth, Boyd Hawes moved to Greece in 1896 to attend the American School of Classical Studies at Athens. At twenty-five, riding a bicycle, skirts blown back in the city breezes, threading her way down Athenian streets, lost in the shadowy wonders of the Acropolis, she was ready to devote herself to archaeology, though first she had to convince the school that no, she really did *not* want to be a librarian.

In time Boyd Hawes revolutionized understandings of local archaeology and chronology on Crete, single-handedly directed excavations for multiple seasons with crews of one hundred men, and made legendary contributions to the emerging science—then more precise and respected than ever—of archaeology.

UNLIKE OTHER WOMEN in this book, who were raised by mothers who encouraged, to some degree, their daughters' independence, Boyd Hawes grew up exclusively in the company of boys. Just a baby when her mother died, Boyd Hawes was raised by her father along with four brothers. She was the youngest, born on October 11, 1871. Her days were filled with playing army soldiers beside her brother Alex; she hardly ever played with dolls or teacups. Alex, the third-youngest sibling, was eleven years her senior and, in the absence of her mother, became a kind of parental figure to Boyd Hawes.

She was a tomboy in skirts. Her hair had been chopped short during a bout of scarlet fever, and as her daughter, Mary, would later recall in her book, Boyd Hawes's "father tried hard to 'rouse domestic tastes' and induce womanliness in his small daughter by having a fine doll's-house built. She secretly liked it with its pretty sets of furniture, but under her brother Allen's martial influence it became a fortress."[4] The dollhouse was occupied by military coup. Happily immersed in games of imaginary war and political intrigue, Boyd Hawes would scramble around and "scout" for the boys. Firefighting was another favorite interest. The whole family loved the fire department—some were even in the business—and they'd delight in going to pyrotechnic shows for fun. A fire alarm would sound through the house, alerting relatives who worked as firemen that they were needed at the station, noise ricocheting off walls, making the five children wild. To match that chaos, the fourth floor of the house was filled with a type of zoo where the children kept a collection of tame pet squirrels that would leap from the tops of doors onto Boyd Hawes's extended arms. Sports and parades, accidents and roughhousing injuries— the Boyd household was a rowdy, happy scene and it was through all this commotion that Boyd Hawes tumbled out a confident, if unconventional, little lady.

Her beloved brother Alex was a formative presence in her life. He introduced her to the study of classics, cheered her along as she entered womanhood, supported her unconditionally, and teased her affectionately about her messy hair and impatient manners. Unfortunately, Alex fell ill and died when he was still a young man. He left Boyd Hawes all of his estate, which she used to finance future endeavors, including college and travel. She was in her last year at Smith College when he died and, deeply grieved by the loss, felt her "heart was not in it [her studies]."⁵ Still, she finished her B.A. in classics (emphasis on Greek) and then had to decide what to do next. She wanted to help those in need and so was torn between teaching and nursing.

Nursing was a recurring interest in Boyd Hawes's life, and sometimes it consumed her whole. Other times, it hovered in the background waiting only to be summoned to return front and center. When her passions were stirred she'd drop everything (her schooling, even her family) to join a war effort. This was not work undertaken down the street, with coffee breaks and a hot bath at night, but work that involved gaining passage on military ships, lying flat on one's back, forbidden to light a match for fear of enemy strike, and traveling great distances to be dropped on the outskirts of a raging battle.

Boyd Hawes never shied from harm's way. She threw herself into her work with the Red Cross and other organizations and devoted her time and superhuman energy to caring for injured and diseased soldiers in the Greco-Turkish War of 1897, the Spanish-American War of 1898, and World War I. She assigned herself selflessly to "death tents,"—where men who had no chance of recovery were taken. There she spoon-fed them milk and arrowroot and changed the dirty straw that served as their mattresses.[6] She was ferociously good at transforming an empty field or abandoned building into an orderly hospital and sorting out the details of receiving medical supplies, delegating staff, and so on. The accolades from government officials and the heartfelt thanks from her patients and their families leave one wondering, a century later, how one could ever do equal good. It's been noted in several accounts of Boyd Hawes's life that her work as a nurse helped her to excel as a field archaeologist. As director of excavations, just as when she was a life-saving nurse, she could transform chaos into order and command the respect of men.

With her instinct for compassion, Boyd Hawes also tried a brief stint of teaching at an impoverished boarding school in North Carolina's "Black Belt," where as a white woman she was in the minority, and not because of her sex. In sharp contrast, her next teaching gig was at a finishing school, where well-to-do girls were groomed for their entrance exams to university.[7] She eventually wearied of teaching pre-college students and decided to pursue her own advanced studies.

Embarking on a grand tour of Europe, in the company of other girls her age, she met the man who tempted her with the open skies of Greece: the place that could "teach you more than you can ever learn in books." When she left for Athens to join the nearly all-male ranks at the American School of Classical Studies on fellowship, she traveled without a chaperone—highly unusual in her day and age. It was almost shocking.

AS AN UNDERGRADUATE student at Smith College, Boyd Hawes had heard Amelia Edwards's lecture *A Thousand Miles Up the Nile*, which was a sensation. Harriet was bitten by the archaeology bug, and now she hoped to pursue active field investigations, which Edwards had described so vividly. There was only one snag in Boyd Hawes's plans: the director of the American School in Athens, through power or influence, kept the women from excavating. Some male professors felt that women shouldn't even be allowed to join class field trips to the country's notable archaeology sites. The physical demands of wielding a pickaxe, even a hand trowel, were seen as not just unladylike but also as strenuously impossible. Ladies just didn't belong in the dirt.

Boyd Hawes was undeterred and fixed on finding a way to put her own shovel in the ground. She'd already concluded that research and libraries were not her destiny. Studying books was tedious, an effort that didn't come easily to her or provide much satisfaction. Although women doing graduate work in archaeology were expected to become librarians, curatorial assistants, or a whole host of other jobs that kept a dress clean and a lady's complexion untouched by a full day's labor in scorching sun, Boyd Hawes knew her "fit" was in the field. A lady who felt best using her hands, busy at work, she liked to see the product of her effort at the end of the day, whether it was soldiers carefully

LEFT: Large vases inscribed with geometric patterns, used in funereal ceremonies
RIGHT: Bracelets, ring, and finely crafted ceramic containers

bandaged and resting in bed or old stonewalls and intact clay pots
etched with vines and octopi lined up in the sun.

ONE SUNDAY MORNING in April 1900, Boyd Hawes awoke
and "lay in bed in one of those delicious dreamy moods when
everything seems possible."[8] Why not try to go to Crete, where
few had ever done any archaeological work? She could make a
real contribution, and she could avoid the pitfalls of trying to
win permission to excavate near Athens (an area already much
claimed by the male faculty at her school). If all went well, she
could make a full expedition. A real chance to dig. She referred
to her plans for expedition as a "campaign," and with luck she
would find a site all her own. This campaign would become the
first of many.

She used all the connections she had, then sought and received
the many permissions required. With some financial backing
from the Archaeological Institute of America and her own

fellowship money, a good deal of support, and a bit of fire in the belly, Boyd Hawes set sail to the Cretan city of Herakleion in the spring of 1900. Her passage was made in a dinghy boat, skipping south across the wine-dark sea to the land fabled in Homer's *Odyssey* to contain ninety ancient cities.[9]

Archaeology in Greece contains layers of history: not just Greek and Roman but a mix of all the diverse strands of cultural influence that comprised the ancient Mediterranean world for thousands of years. Underfoot rests the evidence of lives stretching from Neolithic times to the Early Iron Age and through the Dark Ages. It's a sequence made of broken cups, bones, crushed mosaics, and coins. Harriet wanted to focus on what was then referred to as the pre-Mycenean phase, later to be renamed the Minoan, in large part thanks to her discoveries. It was an early period that dated from 3000 BC to 1450 BC and had originated on Crete.

Boyd Hawes traveled the countryside in search of a site that warranted use of her excavation permit (it could only be used in *one area*, so she had to choose wisely). She traveled by mule and she poked around caves; accommodations were always sorted on the fly. From village to village she inquired about what artifacts the locals might have found while plowing their land. One day, Boyd Hawes's travel companion, a man named Pappadhias, who wore traditional costume made of yards of fabric wrapped around his waist as a skirt, rode on ahead. He always made a fantastic impression, tall and regal, a walking celebration of Cretan pride. When Boyd Hawes arrived she noted, "an altogether exaggerated opinion of our importance had spread throughout the village... Ladies attended by a man in this garb must be great indeed! Soon sealstones, fragments of pottery and bronze would be brought to us quietly, and men would offer to show the fields where these had been unearthed."[10]

She eventually settled on an area recommended to her: the Kavousi region. In need of laborers, she invited men from the nearby village to interview for her workforce. Based on their apparent muscle mass and pleasant demeanor, she selected ten favorites, and with the exception of one, they would remain with her as senior crew for the rest of her archaeological seasons in Greece.[11] Boyd Hawes conducted light excavations at ten sites. By the power of her wheelbarrows, spades, buckets, rope, and workmen's energy, the work was productive. They found a museum's worth of artifacts and could list bronze arrowheads and jewelry, gold leaf, glass, iron swords, vases, spearheads, and a "thin bronze plate engraved with sphinxes, griffins, lions, and human figures" as their inventory.[12] In one location she found an untouched tomb dating to the Iron Age and containing "four skeletons, iron weapons, and over forty vases."[13] No grand palaces or major surprises were unearthed, but the expedition was a steady-handed success. When it was over, Boyd Hawes, proud and proven, returned to the States to lecture and publicize her work.

After hearing Boyd Hawes present her findings from Kavousi at the general meeting of the Archaeological Institute of America in 1900, the secretary of the society, Mrs. Cornelius Stevenson, who held a similar passion for Cretan archaeology,[14] drummed up financial support on behalf of the institute to continue Boyd Hawes's quest (the funding was eventually compromised by bureaucracy, however). She also helped provide the first flicker of international support, as well as an institution on which Boyd Hawes could now depend instead of on her school and fickle fellowships, and most of all, credibility in the eyes of science. Boyd Hawes's career was taking shape.

Impatient for the nickels and dimes to fall into place, Boyd Hawes embarked on her second campaign in the early new year of 1901. She brought a friend, Blanche Wheeler, with her. A former classmate from Smith, Blanche had a background in classical languages and art. The two women made their way to Crete on a ship that "not only pitched and rolled but 'wriggled,'" and they were forced to survive "the stormy seas on a strange, though successful, diet of raw oysters and ice cream."[15] Their journey was three weeks long.

Upon arrival (and likely after a meal that included some solid bread and other non-slippery fare), Boyd Hawes began to comb the landscape once more for the site or sites she would excavate. She was looking for something more substantial than a scattering of tombs, more cohesive than the ten separate sites in Kavousi. She was after a Bronze Age site and ideally a settlement of some kind. The going was not easy. Weather was rough—"thirty-six hours of incessant rain that caused serious floods"—and they were camped in modest little stone huts. These conditions would have been endurable if the archaeology had been good, but that too was looking grim. Every so often Boyd Hawes would stop the donkeys and dismount to examine potsherds littered beneath their hooves. She described their attempts to start minor excavations at sites with a little promise as "meager." And then even her eyes started to play a trickery when

> On holidays and on days when the ground was too wet for digging we rode up and down Kavousi plain and the neighboring coast hill seeking for the bronze-age settlement, which I was convinced lay in the lowlands somewhere near the sea. It was discouraging work for my eyes soon came to see walls and the tops of beehive tombs in every chance grouping of stones and we went to many a rise of ground

which at a distance looked a perfect Mycenean hill, but proved to be all rock." [16]

Nothing worse than day after day of searching for something as small as a buried town in a place as big and open as the sun-baked countryside. Especially on a schedule and budget. Yet she kept at it, hopeful that she would make the great discovery she felt certain was out there.

Rumor of the ladies and their search had circulated around the villages. George Perakis, a local "peasant antiquarian" from the town of Vasiliki, knew of a promising seaside hill where he had collected bits of pottery and seen old walls. As proof, he sent along a nice stone seal from the spot. Boyd Hawes found his story "too interesting to pass unheeded." Wasting no time in visiting the place, they kicked their donkeys to a trot.

She definitely had her site. Surface pottery revealed the curvilinear patterns she knew signified a Bronze Age occupation. Harriet summoned her original crew from the previous campaign and had them bring in more help. Assuming that they could begin a day's work without her, and that all would be slow going as archaeology normally is, Boyd Hawes and Wheeler journeyed to a nearby town so that they could catch up on writing letters. When she returned,

> Men were scattered all over the hillside excitedly clamouring to show their finds—many fragments of vases, a bronze knife, a spear point, house walls and, best of all, a well-paved road with a threshold and a gutter. The workers swelled with pride as, wielding picks and shovels, they amassed basket-loads of history. This was clearly something big and, judging from the pottery, it was of Bronze Age, or Minoan.

The evidence was so promising that Harriet went back to Kavousi and hired fifteen new hands. There was no difficulty in getting them; few could resist the appeal of unknown treasure.[17]

The famous archaeological site of Gournia had been found. The preservation of everyday life was so great that the site was nicknamed "Minoan Pompeii." It was a goldmine, not so much in wealth and treasure as in valuable information. Here was a full settlement where the daily lives of people who farmed and fished, made shoes, wove blankets, made pottery, hammered bronze, carved stone, and looked out to the sea for trade boats and news, could be uncovered and understood. It was a new and critical link in the chronology of Mediterranean archaeology. As the site's significance became increasingly clear, Boyd Hawes rushed to send a telegram to the American Exploration Society. It read: "Discovered Gournia—Mycenaean site, street, houses, pottery, bronzes, stone jars."[18] This was the Eureka moment, her dreams come true.

Gournia eventually encompassed a full three seasons of excavation (1901, 1903, and 1904).[19] Each year Boyd Hawes returned to Crete with her crew of one hundred or more men—and nearly a dozen young girls who helped to wash the potsherds—she worked to piece the architecture and artifacts of the ancient town into a semblance of understanding. She directed the men from morning until night; handled the complicated logistics of digging, mapping, and recording; and oversaw matters such as payroll and means of dissuading the workers from looting. She had reason to be concerned that when her watchful eye was elsewhere, they might pocket and sell off unique finds for a high price. All in all it was a massive effort, one that Boyd Hawes adored while

ABOVE: Hawes in the field in Crete with her assistants and dog

living with her friend Blanche in two rooms near the site, tucked up "over a storehouse at the coastguard station of Pachyammos, which they shared with a colony of rats."[20] Rats didn't matter when you each day were uncovering treasures underfoot.

Boyd Hawes operated on the same principle as Flinders Petrie, whom she visited later in Egypt and who had been so steadfastly supported by Amelia Edwards. Like Petrie, who recognized worth not just in the golden trophy finds but also in the nuts and bolts of more humble sites, Boyd Hawes operated on the principle that history is made by small acts. Yes, the palaces and thrones of antiquity are mighty and beautiful, but the little decorations on potsherds and their changes over time can illuminate the style of a whole society, from rich to poor. The presence or absence of certain types of stone or fishhook styles and the influence of architecture can reveal much more about old trade networks and spheres of influence than a single cache of ruby jewels ever could. In Boyd Hawes's own words, "As of most subjects which deserve any investigation, the more we know the more we want to know. Palaces and tombs are not sufficient; we want also the homes of the people, for without an insight into the life of 'the many' we can not rightly judge the civilization of any period."[21] Boyd Hawes embodied archaeology's turn away from treasure seeking and toward data gathering.

With her finds stacking high, Boyd Hawes was all the more remarkable as an archaeologist because she did two things: first, published her discoveries in timely and thorough fashion, and second, became the first woman invited to lecture for the Archaeological Institute of America. This was major. It announced her stature as a true scientist in a field of men. Her talks were not in the engaging and popular style of Amelia Edwards; they were sharp and technical. Likewise, Boyd Hawes's story of archaeology wasn't told through a lens of emotion. It was more a tale of perseverance and character. The *Philadelphia Public Ledger* of March 5, 1902, reported on Boyd's success at Gournia:

> A woman has shattered another tradition and successfully entered unaided a field hitherto occupied almost exclusively by men, namely archaeological exploration... The results of Miss Boyd's work must be considered remarkable, not only because of their character, but because she achieved them alone. Other women have made names in the fields of archaeological research, but these have done so in company with their husbands, who shared glory with them. But Miss Boyd's work is entirely her own.[22]

In a similar vein, Mrs. Stevenson commented: "So few women have achieved distinction as field archaeologists that Miss Boyd's success must be greeted with peculiar pride by Americans... it was reserved to an American woman to undertake

ABOVE: The field crew at Gournia, including Boyd Hawes and Blanche Wheeler (second row from the front, first and second from the right)

singlehandedly the business responsibility and scientific conduct of an expedition."[23]

They missed mention of Zelia Nuttall, but she was so rooted in Mexico, and her childhood such a patchwork of European cities, that her American story was diluted. Boyd Hawes's work energized U.S. patriotism. And while not altogether accurate to say an American was the first woman to conduct an archaeological expedition—Gertrude Bell, a Brit, did that by herself too—Boyd Hawes was the first to lead a full-scale excavation alone, without an archaeologist spouse by her side or a team of other trained archaeologists. Her position as a true pioneer in the field was applauded. The accolades kept coming. Her publications were highly regarded. Would she remain a bright and historic star in the canons of archaeological history and its scholars, or not?

Throughout her excavations at Gournia, Boyd Hawes brought in assistants and provided them with some of the best in field excavation training. Two of those colleagues were Richard Berry

ABOVE: Diggers at Gournia, where a tremendous number of artifacts and archaeological features were uncovered

Seager and Edith Hall, another Smith graduate who would soon make a name for herself in archaeology. Some later publications would, outrageously, credit the young man Seager with the discovery and excavation of Gournia. Others would describe the work as a joint collaboration between Boyd Hawes and Seager. With the passage of time, Boyd Hawes's breakthrough accomplishments were clouded, erased in places, and slighted. She would one day reflect on "having learned how easily women's acts are ascribed to men or completely wiped out." [24] Boyd Hawes didn't hesitate to point out the facts very, very clearly. She had found the buried city. The excavation permit was in her name. Gournia was, as archaeology sites go, all hers.

"HUNT DEAD CITIES AND FIND LOVE." [25] That's what one of the newspaper headlines shouted when Boyd Hawes announced her engagement to British anthropologist Charles Henry Hawes in 1905. He had come to visit Gournia while touring the region to measure people's heads in hopes of determining the origins of races. Harriet and Henry's first meeting on site was uneventful (she gave him a quick tour), but later they found each other again on a boat headed to Greece. Their daughter notes that though this meeting was a crucial turning point, "they did not speak of marriage, except the 'captive' variety, and then strictly in anthropological terms."[26] Boyd Hawes was thirty-four years old, and Henry wanted to marry her. She liked him too.

They wed in a small ceremony at an Episcopal church on March 3, 1906. Nine months later, Alexander Boyd was born, and four years after that daughter Mary (future author of her mother's biography) joined the family. Out of the dusty field, Boyd Hawes was now very much in the kitchen. She had two young children to look after, a husband, meals to make, a house to tend—and a massive publication on her archaeological excavations at Gournia to complete and publish. She pulled this off before Alex could walk, but it was taxing and she had to adjust to juggling her professional passions with the domestic duties she had signed on for. Her daughter would note that "the role of housewife was totally out of character for Harriet" and that "stories of her domestic efforts became legendary." She forgot her babies in their carriages while she shopped, cooked ambitious menus with unfortunate results, and found housework to be almost offensive, not because a person shouldn't be clean and make their home a pleasant place, but because men were not asked or expected to do the same. Boyd Hawes had skillfully dealt with large-scale wartime nursing efforts and complex cultural stratigraphy, but a "domestic goddess" she was not.

In spite of the trials (and surely the triumphs too) that Boyd Hawes faced in this next chapter of her life, she reminds us that *she* made the choices for herself; society did not. At the age of thirty-five, she had already passed the normal marrying age; between 1900 and 1910 the average age of the American bride was just shy of twenty-two.[27] A nonconformist, Boyd Hawes had a successful career and the means to support herself. Her marriage to Henry didn't provide materials comforts, as he was a struggling anthropologist and university lecturer who had much to offer by way of intellectual stimulation but much less in the way of financial support. They struggled to make ends meet. Boyd Hawes had married for love and because she wanted a family. She believed that women's work should be viewed not as duty or humdrum routine, but as art. It was, as she called it, "the art of living," and even when dinner was burning black, she became an active advocate for the worth of a woman's work in all its variations.[28]

YEARS LATER, IN 1925, BOYD HAWES meditated more deeply on the choice women face between career and motherhood. If "choice" is not quite the word—at least for the majority of women at the turn of the twentieth century—then it could be simply called the shared predicament. Can a woman be a pioneer—a convention-crushing rebel who succeeds in a man's world against all odds—and still sing lullabies to her children at night? The question is as old as an archaeological site.

Boyd Hawes summarized her thoughts about this question: "A woman should expect her intellectual life to be interrupted, i.e., she should prepare to give the first 10 years after marriage... to her family interests... Perhaps she can keep alive her intellectual interests and return to them with new zest and judgment after the ten years."[29]

Perhaps? It's as though a sigh escapes between the lines. After her marriage, Boyd Hawes's fieldwork in Greece did stop, though she continued to publish. She and Henry co-authored a famous little book called *Crete the Forerunner of Greece;* it received rave reviews and was heralded as "a milestone in the progress of popular acquaintance with results of archaeological research."[30] So while her intellectual interests persisted and found an outlet through the pen, she relinquished her days of digging. One has to wonder how much she missed them.

Forever a volcano, Boyd Hawes eventually threw herself into social issues and politics with the same gusto she had brought to archaeology. She nursed overseas again, leaving her children in the care of a nanny when necessary. And she became more and more devoted to cause of justice and international peace. She never lost her burning urgency to act, and although archaeology was a major chapter, it was truly just one of the many remarkable chapters that made up the story of her life.

Boyd Hawes concluded her thoughts on the decision to be a wife and mother by saying that a woman's "happiness in accepting this interruption will depend largely on her having anticipated it as part of the Good Life."[31] An "interruption" it may have been, but Harriet Boyd Hawes embraced as much living as any person, man or woman, ever could. Never a second wasted, her life was a good one. She died in March 1945, recipient of the first honorary doctorate for her work at Gournia, awarded by her alma mater Smith College, and hero to the multitude of women archaeologists who would follow in her rumbling wake.

ABOVE: Agatha Christie, famous mystery novel writer, circa 1925

AGATHA CHRISTIE

· · · · ·

ARCHAEOLOGY'S

Big Detective

"'All by yourself?' said Carlo, slightly doubtful. 'All by yourself to the Middle East? You don't know anything about it.'

"'Oh, that will be all right,' I said. 'After all, one must do things by oneself sometime, mustn't one?'"[1]

Agatha Christie, the world-famous mystery writer, then thought quietly to herself: "It's now or never. Either I cling to everything that's safe and that I know, or else I develop initiative, do things own my own."[2] She chose the latter path and booked a train ticket on the Orient Express. It was a journey that would lead her to two new loves: her second husband, Sir Max Mallowan, and archaeology.

This new chapter in Christie's life began when she was forty years old. The woman with a detective's heart brushed herself off after the loss of her mother, an unwanted divorce, and a spell of illness that she believed was the precursor to a nervous breakdown and an episode of amnesia. Always a dreamer, and always on a path closely wrapped around family, Christie broke free from an environment of long-standing familiarity to try something new. Her career as an internationally acclaimed mystery writer was still in its early stages. She was writing her first books, and they were selling well, but it was only when she lost nearly everything dear to her that she realized her desire for adventure and was able to reach her full potential.

Her autobiography begins in the field. She anchored the first page of her six-hundred-page meandering life story in the place she loved best: a canvas tent beside the excavation trenches. With a handmade sign written in cuneiform posted to the door, her tent was called BEIT AGATHA (Agatha's House) and was located at an archaeological site in Nimrud, Iraq. Only ten feet square, the floor was covered with rush mats and coarse rugs. From the window she could see the snowy mountains of Kurdistan. Tucked into her private abode, she could focus on her writing. But as she described it, once "the dig proceeds there will probably be no time for this. Objects will need to be cleaned and repaired. There will be photography, labeling, cataloguing and packing" of artifacts.[3] For the famed author with more books sold and translated than any other author in the world (except the Bible), archaeology came first. She loved it.

Christie lived and worked in the East, particularly in Syria and Iraq, between 1928 and 1958. Thirty years spent in the field! Captivated by the natural similarities between a detective's work and archaeology, she wrote three crime stories infused with the flavor of her travels and archaeological prowess: *Murder on the Orient Express, Death on the Nile,* and *Appointment with Death.* Another autobiographical work, *Come, Tell Me How You Live,* chronicles three seasons spent excavating a number of tells in Syria. The tagline hollers: BOARD THE ORIENT EXPRESS FOR

SYRIA—AND ENCHANTED MEMORIES OF EXOTIC LANDS! Light, humorous, and self-deprecating, the book is also a testament to Agatha's real understanding of the archaeological process and her own contributions to it.

Christie discovered archaeology through her own initiative— she boarded the train to visit acquaintances at the site of Ur—but it was romantic love that brought her much closer to it. While at Ur, she was introduced to the young Max Mallowan, fourteen years her junior and an assistant to the site's lead archaeologist. The two quickly became friends and were sent off together, he as her appointed guide, to see the sights. Against a backdrop of desert sandstorms, flashfloods, crushed potsherds, and late trains the duo enjoyed an unusual and unsuspected courtship.

"I AM TODAY the same person as that solemn little girl with pale flaxen sausage-curls" wrote Christie in her seventies.[4] That little girl was born September 15, 1890, in the seaside town of Torquay, off the Devon coast in England. The sausage curls eventually grew out into hair so long she could sit on it, and the little girl became a bit less "solemn" as she matured. Christie's childhood days set the stage for a life filled by wild imagination and the propensity to get lost in fictional worlds. It started with invisible kittens and horses and hula hoops cast as swirling sea dragons in the early years and was later followed up with murderers, victims, scheming plots, and a legendary Belgian detective by the name of Hercule Poirot.

Christie had by her own account been privileged with the greatest streak of luck life can afford: a happy childhood. Her father, Frederick Alvah Miller, was an American; born into money, he was "lazy" because he didn't work but loved because he was so unconditionally pleasant and full of easy humor. Her mother, Clarissa Margaret Boehme, was a trickier creature, whom Christie described as having an "enigmatic and arresting personality—more forceful than my father—startlingly original in her ideas, shy and miserable about herself, and at the bottom, I think, a natural melancholy."[5] Together, though, the two had a happy marriage, something that Christie recognized even as a child, and ultimately something she would want very much as a woman.

There were two other Miller children. Christie's brother, Monty, was a livewire, capricious and difficult, unable to reach any social milestones of success (in his day that was marriage and money), but he served in the military abroad, settled in Uganda, had a thunderously good time all the way through, and died of a bad leg when he was middle-aged. Christie's sister, Madge, was beautiful and had sparkling conversation. It was always Madge who wrote the best stories, did well in school, and had every boy in town smitten with her. By contrast, Christie was secretive and shy.

Both her siblings were sent away for an education, while Christie was left to roam about Ashfield, the family home, raised by her mother, gossipy grandmothers, nurses, and a team of cooks and servants who coddled her. As the youngest, Christie was given free reign because her mother had concluded that "the best way to bring up girls was to let them run wild as much as possible; to give them good food, fresh air, and not to force their minds in anyway."[6] This thinking only applied to girls. Boys needed a real education. But Mrs. Miller didn't think that girls or boys should learn how to read until they were eight or so—it would spoil their minds, hamper their development. In love with books and impatient to understand the words they were made of, Christie taught herself to read. This was one of the ways she entertained herself: lost in her father's library, absorbed by the musty pages of his leather bound books.

Her upbringing was very Victorian; she was taught to be a delicate thing or at least to pretend she was. Her grandmothers would hammer it home that fainting fits, extreme sensitivity, lack of appetite, and an early onset of consumption (a chronic bloody cough now commonly referred to as tuberculosis) were fashionable. Love and romance were bound up in tragedy and the potential for premature, and therefore gut-wrenching, death. Girls should always be on the brink of perishing.

From most people's point of view, Victorian days were a dark time for women's rights. In Christie's eyes, however, the ladies were having a laugh. In establishing themselves as the "weaker sex," Christie said, "[Victorian women] got their menfolk where they wanted them. They established their frailty, delicacy, sensibility—their constant need of being protected and cherished. Did they lead miserable, servile lives, downtrodden and oppressed? Such is not *my* recollection..."[7]

Her outlook harkens back to Jane Dieulafoy's view of marriage wherein a woman's happiness and purpose is achieved through selfless devotion to her spouse: "A woman, when she marries," explains Christie, "accepted as her destiny *his* place in the world and *his* way of life." She concludes, "That seems to me sound sense and the foundation of happiness."[8] Coming from the pen of one of the world's most professionally successful women, a lady who has sold something like four *billion* books in her career, the view is a curious one. Christie could hardly be corralled into anyone's definition of a supposed "weaker sex." Then again, she cheerfully likened her own disposition to that of a loyal dog, and dogs rarely mind the master's leash if it means they'll get a good walk.

The Miller family hit difficult times when Christie was eleven. Her father died, and because his estate had been poorly managed by the banks, money was suddenly scarce and the upper-class comforts of lavish meals and domestic servants took a hit. Things were scaled back. Christie's mother navigated the family through these challenges with her common sense, and Christie made clear that while the Miller family was always comfortable, they were not rich. She and her sister rarely attended a party if it was too far to walk to because carriages and horses were expensive. A girl could have beautiful silk evening dresses, but she would have only two or three at most, and those would have to last at least a year. Butlers and doormen were nice but far from necessary. A cook and a maid, however, were as essential as bread and milk on the table; they would be the last things to let go of.

When Christie had reached the age of seventeen, her mother was obliged to arrange the season of her "coming out." Normally, a girl's first season was hosted in the parlors and at the parties of London—a family would demonstrate its wealth, social standing, and all-around good graces through the charm of their daughter. She would be entertained and toured or whirled and wooed by men seeking a wife, and her parents would scrutinize the options. Christie's sister, Madge, went out in fine style when the family had more money, but left to her own resources, their mother had to devise a more affordable season for her second daughter.

She decided that Christie would go to Cairo. Unlike Madge, Christie was shy and far from fluent in the art of flirtation. In Egypt she would be "familiarised with dancing, talking to young men, and all the rest of it," and Christie thus arrived, quickly enchanted. She said Cairo was a "dream of delight." Outfitted in a dress of shot pale pink satin with a bunch of pink rosebuds gathered to one shoulder, Christie went to five dances each week. She and her mother stayed "on tour" three whole months.

Christie's confidence grew in Cairo; she nabbed one marriage proposal that her mother declined for her, and she arrived at the conclusion that she was a good-looking and desirable young woman. Her coming-out season had made her blossom, and she'd been introduced to society with all the bang and buck a girl could want. What she had *not* been introduced to was all the Egyptian archaeology around her.

Her mother tried coaxing her out to see the museums and nearby ruins, but Christie protested and fussed. Her mind was on piano music and picnics. In hindsight, she was relieved to have missed the antiquities of Egypt as a girl: "I am very glad she [Christie's mother] did not take me. Luxor, Karnak, the beauties of Egypt, were to come upon me with wonderful impact about twenty years later. How it would have spoilt them for me if I had seen them with unappreciative eyes."[9] Egypt ushered Christie out of her shell and into a new phase of life as a young woman with options and appeal. In time, she would return the favor.

IN THE MEANTIME, Christie had a heavy set of domestic duties to attend to. Come 1914, like nearly all the young women of the time, she became a nurse during World War I. She wasn't especially ambitious about pursuing a career, and in between her days of bandaging the wounded, she broke a few hearts. Several marriage proposals came her way, but she turned them down. The first one she accepted was from a man named Reggie. He was significantly older than her and managed to attract the fickle Christie through a kind of reverse psychology, intended or not. Instead of pleading that she accept his offer, he suggested that she take her time to think about it and encouraged her to keep going to parties, keep meeting other men, keep her mind open. His patience made Christie very impatient and more determined than ever to marry him. He left for service (a two-year stint), and although they wrote letters constantly, her desire for someone inclined to act with bit more passion and even a dash of jealousy grew. Her wish was soon granted by the arrival of the stormier Archibald (Archie) Christie, who flew airplanes for the Royal Flying Corps. His approach was more intense: I love you; I must marry you, *now*. She liked it. Her engagement to Reggie was called off, and her engagement with Archie was on, if protracted, for he had no money. Although both of their parents blessed the couple's intention to wed, it was agreed that Archie had to fluff up the nest and earn at least some of his fortune first. They were separated by the war, jobs were tough to come by, and they were victims of a capricious game of love: could they succeed against the odds? The back-and-forth was grueling—there were constant breakups and makeups—until one day just before Christmas in 1914 they ran off to the equivalent of city hall and got hitched in the afternoon. Enter Mrs. Agatha Christie.

The Christies were a young, happy, struggling couple. Archie returned from the war and decided to leave flying behind in favor of an office job. Agatha began to write her mysteries and by 1920 was a newly published author. Just before that, after a stretch of nausea in which Agatha felt like she was aboard a "nine-month ocean voyage to which you never get acclimatized"[10] she gave birth to a baby girl, Rosalind. It was a time of cheer and high spirits; the bills were paid on time and her little family was in good health. And the Christies had a pretty flat in London.[11]

Christie's success as a writer kept growing too, as did the speed of her prolific pen. She turned out at least one book a year, sometimes three. While everything in her life was coasting along on an even keel, Archie was invited to travel around the world as part of the Empire Tour to showcase "products of the British Empire." Archie's job was to handle the finances while interest was being drummed up in the various provinces and territories of Australia,

ABOVE: Christie and her young daughter, Rosalind

New Zealand, Canada, and South Africa. Much to Agatha's delight, they could add a month's holiday in Honolulu to the trip. They packed their bags and left in January 1922. Rosalind went to stay with Agatha's mother and sister.

While on tour, Christie found out that she was an international hit; her reputation had preceded her. People loved her books, and Archie stood by and watched as the flames of his wife's fame grew hotter. When they returned from abroad, Archie had to find a new job. Over the next few years, the only steady factor in the couple's life was Christie's rising star as a professional writer. One biographer notes that at age thirty-four she had reached a point when her "health and strength, looks and temper were at their most resilient, when it is easy to feel sure of one's own nature and capacities."[12] That resiliency would be sorely tested in a few years' time, when Archie announced that he was in love with a golfing girl.

The year 1926 was one that Agatha would forever "hate recalling. As so often in life, when one thing goes wrong everything goes wrong," she remarked. The series of misfortunes began with the death of her mother. Archie missed the funeral because he was in Spain. When he returned, he was anxious to get away from any unhappiness and suggested that Christie leave her family home and go away with him. She declined, finding his cheer-up attitude "very hard to bear when you have lost a person who is one of three you love best in the world."[13] He left, and she stayed behind to sort out the estate at Ashfield. Christie fell into a deep despair; she would burst into tears for no reason and forget her own name when signing checks. She was tired. Too tired. Archie returned just as her spirits were lifting a little, but when he arrived he was a stranger. She likened the feeling to a waking nightmare. He soon announced that he had fallen in love with a lady named Nancy and that he'd like a divorce as soon as possible. "I suppose" she writes, that "with those words, that part of my life—my happy, successful, confident life—ended."[14]

The author's disappearance followed. Distressed, she left the house on a December evening, driving off without a word to the housemaids about where she was headed. Her car was later found abandoned, halfway down a grassy slope and buried in some bushes. The media went wild. Christie had vanished, and a massive eleven-day manhunt ensued. There were accusations that she had been murdered by Archie, that she had devised her own mysterious publicity stunt, that she'd committed suicide or been terribly hurt. Search teams roamed the countryside, lakes and ponds were dredged in gruesome hope of finding her body, and bloodhounds barked as they tried to pick up a scent. All the while, Christie had checked herself into a spa hotel. Drinking coffee and eating Melba toast with grapefruit slices, she read the daily newspaper headlines about her own disappearance, but she did not know they were referring to her. The depression she had been suffering from had culminated in some kind of nervous breakdown and amnesia. She lost herself, literally. The whole event was traumatic, and Christie was subsequently mortified by the media's ongoing feeding frenzy.

Things eventually calmed down, and she granted Archie the divorce she didn't want. She left with Rosalind for the Canary Islands, hopeful that she could catch her breath there and get some writing done. When she returned home to England, she was in a much more adventurous, lost-it-all-anyway mood.

CHRISTIE'S CAREER IN archaeology was unconventional. Although she had "always been faintly attracted to archaeology," unlike the other pioneers in this book, she didn't pursue it as her own career. Instead, she was a unique kind of *witness* to the field. She was fluent in archaeological methods and sites, yet she never published any of her own research or excavation results. She was an assistant, an observer, a field hand, the wife of the director. Her contributions to archaeology are not as much groundbreaking in the academic sense as they are captivating, highlighted by good old-fashioned mystery, and successful in exciting public interest in ancient landscapes and antiquity. Who could be better qualified to reconstruct events of the past than a mystery writer who has an eye peeled for every clue?

Christie met Leonard and Katherine Woolley on the famous site of Ur in Iraq (a site Gertrude Bell was once involved with). She traveled there via the Orient Express and by boat to Beirut, suffering from the agony of greasy food and bedbug bites so bad she had to cut the sleeves of her shirt to let her swollen arms out. Leonard was the site's director and Katherine the charismatic and mildly crazy wife who also happened to be a huge fan of Christie's book *The Murder of Roger Ackroyd*. She invited Christie to visit and made sure she received VIP treatment. While most visitors to an archaeological site were viewed as pesky interruptions, Christie was warmly received. Leonard gave her a tour through the excavations, and she met with other historians and scholars as well.

Her time at Ur was transformative. She wrote:

> I fell in love with Ur, with its beauty in the evenings, the ziggurat standing up, faintly shadowed, and the wide sea of sand with its lovely pale colors of apricot, rose, blue and mauve changing every minute. I enjoyed the workmen, the foremen, the little basket boys, the pickmen—the whole technique and life. The lure of the past came up to grab me ... The carefulness of lifting pots and objects from the soil filled me with a longing to be an archaeologist myself." [15]

That longing would come to fruition. While on site, Christie also met the man she would fall in love with—Max Mallowan, a "thin, dark, young man" and a true archaeologist who would reach renown in his lifetime. He was then twenty-five years old (at age forty, Christie had a little streak of cougar in her) and an invaluable assistant to Leonard. He oversaw the field crew, which numbered two hundred and above, spoke Arabic, organized the books, and knew how to handle the irascible Katherine (methods included hair brushing, massage, and placing a few blood-sucking leeches here and there at her request[16]). After a brief return to England, Christie went back to Ur the following season to view the progress in the excavation trenches and then travel through Syria and Greece. Her arrival was greeted by a vicious sandstorm and Max. Katherine Woolley declared that Max would be escorting Christie to Nejef, Kerbala, the site of Nippur, and finally on to Baghdad, setting them on a path neither would have expected. Christie balked; after three months of excavating a young man wouldn't want to spend his free time touring her around. Would he?

Max didn't mind at all it, and besides, once Katherine made a decision about something, there was no undoing it. They started off, and under Max's influence Christie became "more enamored of digging than ever."[17] As they traveled together, Agatha would pick up potsherds from all the tell sites they visited. She was most enchanted by the brilliantly colored pieces—the green, turquoise, blue, and gold-flecked bits that would have sat well in a peacock's tail—and she collected a large bag of them. When they reached a hotel in Baghdad, Christie dipped each sherd in water and "arranged them in glistening iridescent patterns of colour" on the floor. The result was an archaeological rainbow. Max added a few pieces of his own to the display, and Agatha caught him staring at her "with the air of an indulgent scholar looking kindly at a foolish but not unlikeable child . . ."[18]

During their travels together Max realized that Christie was wonderful. When their car got badly stuck in sand after the two had snuck away for a quick swim in their improvised swimsuits of doubled-up "knickers," they faced the prospect of a day or two in the desert stranded without water. Max's response was to get busy solving the problem; Christie decided to take a nap. It was her mellow nonchalance toward a rather urgent situation that made Max realize she was the woman for him. They parted ways in Baghdad, but soon enough he found his way to England, where he looked her up. They met for breakfast. She invited him to come stay at Ashfield for a weekend. They got along so fabulously well as friends that she was struck dumb when he proposed marriage.

Max snuck into her bedroom and sat at the edge of her bed to ask if she might marry him. He also asked if she minded that his profession was "digging up the dead." The woman whose very favorite thing was a well-done murder replied, not at all—"I adore corpses and stiffs." [19]

Christie said it was through friendship that Max made his way into her heart. Had she known that he was courting romance, she would have turned away from it. Her divorce had been bitterly painful, shameful, and her desire to remarry—to risk being hurt again—was nil. But there was Max, the twenty-something stealth who had managed to slip past the clever mystery writer's

ABOVE: Christie and her husband Max Mallowan on their archaeological journey to northern Iraq

instinct for foreshadowing. She could think of every reason why they shouldn't marry, but she couldn't say that she didn't want to, because it wasn't true. When she thought about it, she realized that "nothing in the world would be as delightful as being married to him." In 1930, Agatha Christie married the young archaeologist in an Edinburgh church.

BY 1934, THE COUPLE WAS IN the Khabur valley, in the northeastern portion of Syria, scouting for tells. They circled the bases of some sixty mounds to sniff out the most promising one for prehistoric pottery. Walking around and around, staring at the ground looking for just the right kind of potsherds, Christie began "to understand why archaeologists have a habit of walking with eyes downcast to the ground." With a long season ahead of her, she said that "soon, I feel, I myself shall forget to look around me, or out to the horizon. I shall walk looking down at my feet as though there only an interest lies."[20]

They settled on the tell site of Chagar Bazar, and a lifestyle of *le camping* began. The phrase amused Christie. While en route to their survey of tells, she, Max, and the architect they had brought along to map the cities and towns they hoped to uncover stumbled upon some French tourists. The tourists were fascinated by the band of traveling archaeologists, and the ladies inquired about Christie's accommodations: *Ah, Madame, vous faites le camping?* Christie thought the expression classified their adventure as pure sport. Yes, *le camping* it was, albeit *sans* tent. They settled into a mouse-infested ("Mice across one's face, mice tweaking your hair—mice! Mice! MICE! . . .") mud-brick building. The services of a "highly professional cat" were immediately solicited and took care of the mouse problem, but it wasn't until the walls had been whitewashed, the windowsills and doors painted, and a smattering of furniture brought in that the couple felt comfortable and Christie, after weeks, could finally wash her hair.

By night Max and Agatha reckoned with armies of cockroaches and zingy fleas, but nothing was so bad as the mice. A schedule slowly fell into place. Max got up at dawn and made his way to the excavations. Christie would either go with him or see to the mending of pottery and objects and the labeling of artifacts, and every so often she would make use of the typewriter she'd lugged halfway around the world.[21]

Work at Chagar Bazar was conducted from 1935 to 1938, and during that time, Christie's involvement with the excavations continually deepened. One account notes that "she had developed into an indispensable member of the team, leaving her own career as a writer in abeyance."[22] While living and working in the field, she wore several hats. She oversaw matters pertaining to the kitchen and tried to teach the hired hands to cook everything from omelets to lemon curd to soufflés. Her previous work as a nurse put her in a good position to function as a sort of *ad hoc* desert medicine woman; not only did she treat the injured field crew, but she would also give counsel (and aspirin) to the Kurdish and Arab women who came to see her in groups all dressed in their flowing robes and jingling bangles. She supervised the basket boys, the table settings, the shopping excursions, and the purchase of meat. Yet she also began to play a critical role in the archaeology that was being conducted, and her coat pockets were always bulging with the potsherds she loved to collect.

Christie first became acquainted with the process of artifact collection and cleaning while working with Max at the site of Nimrud. Beginning work in 1949, Max would continue to excavate the site for the next ten years. There Christie spruced up the ancient ivory carvings that were eventually dispersed to

museums around the world and even fabricated her own toolkit
for dealing with them:

> I had my part in cleaning them. I had my own favourite
> tools, just as any professional would: an orange stick, pos-
> sibly a very fine knitting needle—one season a dentist's tool,
> which he lent, or rather gave me—and a jar of cosmetic face-
> cream which I found more useful than anything else for gen-
> tly coaxing the dirt out of the crevices without harming the
> friable ivory. In fact there was such a run on my face-cream
> that there was nothing left for my poor old face after a couple
> of weeks![23]

Agatha Christie pioneered a whole new method in artifact
processing: a cold-cream wash. The stuff that smoothed facial
wrinkles was equally effective at restoring a fine polish to ivory.

While working, Christie would reflect on the "patience, the
care that was needed; the delicacy of touch" that her task required.
She devoted herself to archaeology with ease because for her it
was a life "free of outside shadows."[24] Her books would still be
written—and she loved to write them—but she surrendered to
archaeology's simplicity, to the uncomplicated and predictable
routines of dig life. She didn't envy the site director's job—scanning the whole site, putting this and that together, assessing what
fit with what and where the next trench should be opened—but
rather very much enjoyed the workmen's lifestyle. Freed from
Victorian society, career strains, and a million places to be, she
reveled in a simpler life: eat breakfast (hot tea and eggs); walk
the site; complete multiple tasks that can be started, finished, and
savored with a feeling of satisfaction; have dinner, some wine,
and a biscuit; go to bed, and start the next day anew and in the
same way. Life on a dig was rigorous and not always comfortable,

but it was also devoid of the chaos or social obligations that the naturally shy Christie was inclined to avoid. Field days were the "most perfect" she had ever known.

Standing in a vast and quiet desert landscape, sipping her tea, Christie mused that five thousand years ago, this had been *the* busy part of the world: a thriving region of commerce, trade, and bustling temples. She considered the dainty china cup in her hand and its long evolution: "Here [during their survey of tells] were the beginnings of civilization, and here, picked up by me, this broken fragment of a clay pot, hand made, with a design of dots and cross-hatching in black paint, is the forerunner of the Woolworth cup out of which this very morning I have drunk my tea..."[25]

Everything in her excavator's life was akin to a jigsaw puzzle. She fit the pieces together. From reassembling broken potsherds into a whole pot to making connections between the material cultures of then and now, Christie reveled in the hints and revelations of archaeology. It was during this first season at Chagar Bazar that Agatha felt some writerly inspiration as well and wrote *Murder in Mesopotamia,* in which an archaeologist's wife, highly reminiscent of Katherine Woolley, is murdered.

The second season of work at Chagar Bazar took place in 1936, and Christie began photographing the dig and the objects recovered. She even made two 16-mm films, each forty-five minutes long, which recorded both the technical side of excavating and the humorous anecdotes of everyday life on an archaeological site.[26] Her job was to take highly accurate pictures of the artifacts found—each detail in clear relief, with a scale alongside the object. She had her own little darkroom where she would work—and little it was. She wrote that "in it, one can neither sit nor stand! Crawling in on all fours, I develop plates, kneeling with bent head. I come out practically asphyxiated with heat and unable to stand upright."[27] She craved a little sympathy for the suffering she endured in her chemical-filled hotbox, but Max and the others were far more interested in the quality of the negatives than the photographer's comfort, or lack thereof.

The second season of work in Syria was also when Max decided to open excavations of two tells simultaneously. They continued their work at Chagar Bazar and began new investigations at the nearby Tell Brak. In between seasons they had returned home for a visit. Max wrote up his archaeological reports while Christie luxuriated in her fill of "Devon, of red rocks and blue sea... [her] daughter, the dog, the bowls of Devonshire cream, apples, bathing..."[28] Now back in the field, Max and Agatha had the pleasure of a new house to live in at Chagar Bazar (one with a more spacious darkroom), and they were armed with restored

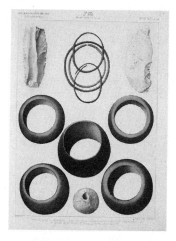 

LEFT: Bronze bracelets, decorative rings, and simple stone tools
RIGHT: Carved spear points found in a burial site

ABOVE: The young writer Agatha Christie, 1924

energy and six rounds of ripe Camembert cheese. As a side note, the cheese was sadly misplaced and lost in the back of a cupboard, and it wasn't until the house was pungent with a smell they likened to death that they found the "gluey odorous mass" and decided to bury it in a remote spot, far from the house. It was back to hot tea, hard bread, and eggs.

Work at the two tells carried on through a third season, and it was only because war broke out in 1939 that excavations at the Tell Brak, a site Max thought worthy of decades of investigation, would stop. Both Chagar Bazar and Tell Brak were, in Max's mind, of "extraordinary interest archaeologically, historically and artistically."[29] Each had its major discoveries. At Chagar Bazar they found a burnt-out palace containing about seventy cuneiform tablets that revealed much about the ethnic backgrounds of the former residents. Tell Brak contained, among many other things, the spectacular Eye Temple, named for the "hundreds of little eye idols of black and white alabaster that lay all over the floors."[30] Throughout all of the work, Christie was in lockstep with her archaeologist husband; she took part in every aspect of field life for many years afterwards. Christie's last dig occurred when she was sixty-eight. She and Max were still married and excavating Nimrud.

CHRISTIE'S FAMOUS LITERARY creation, the detective Hercule Poirot, explains his approach to crime solving in *Death on the Nile:*

> Once I went professionally to an archaeological expedition—
> and I learnt something there. In the course of an excavation,
> when something comes out of the ground, everything is
> cleared away very carefully all around it. You take away the

loose earth, and you scrape here and there with a knife until finally your object is there, all alone, ready to be drawn and photographed with no extraneous matter confusing it. That is what I have been seeking to do—clear away the extraneous matter so that we can see the truth—the naked shining truth."[31]

Christie's love and knowledge of archaeology—such a little known fact about her life—shaped much of her writing. You could say that the archaeological process was at the heart of things. Cleaning away the fluff and confusion that clouds a good story, Christie stabbed at the moment of discovery with all the precision of a carefully wielded spade. She honed her trade through the typewriter while hip-deep in the excavation trenches.

All archaeologists are detectives of the past: they reconstruct events from the clues given in crumbling foundations, a lost gold earring, or the fragment of an inscription. To decipher what happened in a place thousands of years ago requires all the skill and cunning of a private investigator. For what is archaeology if not mystery? And where would archaeology be without the deft literary hand of a great mystery writer?

Agatha Christie was never a proper archaeologist per se; she was never a field director and had no academic publications or university affiliation. But she was its champion and its practitioner. She introduced her readers to the thrills of archaeology—its landscape and its ruins. She also brought her readers into the mind of archaeology, inviting them to interpret the evidence and think critically about a sequence of events, about how one thing leads to another. Christie always felt that she and Max were an excellent match, personally and professionally. The mystery writer and the archaeologist had a lot in common.

The field, the Orient, was where Christie felt she belonged. Although she delighted in spending time back home in England, a bowl of cream in easy reach and a white porcelain tub with hot water at her ready, the desert was her happiness. The stuff of her dreams. Archaeology made her life more beautiful than before. One gray winter in London, still enchanted by the memory of soft desert colors, Christie commissioned a special pair of pajamas for herself. Made of crêpe de chine, the bottoms were apricot like sand and the top was blue like sky.[32] The mystery writer who devoted thirty years of her life to archaeological fieldwork wrapped herself up in the beauty of a Middle Eastern desert and slept in the colors of its sunrise.

ABOVE: The accomplished Dorothy Garrod, 1913

DOROTHY GARROD

· · · · ·

LIKE A GLASS OF

Stony White Wine

By the late 1920s, archaeology had evolved from a passionate (even personal) pursuit of the past to a purer science. The field had matured since Amelia Edwards boarded her *dahabeeyeh* and Gertrude Bell explored uncharted deserts alone. The lush travel narratives that described archaeological expedition as adventure were fading away. They became less popular, less useful to a science reaching for ever more precise answers. In the early twentieth century there was a new voice for archaeology, and it was Dorothy Garrod.

Take the following as an example. In the passage below Garrod offers a technical description of wind-borne sands that would have inspired Amelia's pen to heady prose musing on those bits of ancient earth snatched by a swinging gale, bound in heavenly light. Garrod was a little more straightforward: "The sands and travertines at Devil's Tower are clearly wind-borne. Apart from their contents the way in which layer 1 was driven up against the face of the rock and into the roof of the fissure demonstrates this beyond question."[1]

Here was the new tone of archaeology—concise and clear, grounded in facts, leanly expressed. Objective. The older accounts of the field that melded travelogue and discovery in equal measure were laid to rest, relegated to literary artifact. They were appreciated to be sure (they were the written foundations of the field), but personal memoir no longer had a place in an archaeological survey report.

In the beginning archaeology served the personal taste of the researcher; it was a kind of intellectual pursuit sidesaddled to the exotic. Now archaeology was the thing served; served by scientists willing to leave out any mention of themselves. The spotlight shone exclusively on a site, the evidence found, and the conclusions drawn. Archaeology was suddenly selfless. People were still proud to put their names on reports, build reputable careers, and drum up recognition for their scholarly finesse, but the stories of individual experience and romance were relegated to the discipline's backwaters. The goal had shifted from entertainment to information testing and building.

Archaeology had at last dug out its place as a credible international science. With so much evidence coming to light, ranging from buried towns like Gournia to ancient bones that revealed the intricacies of our human evolution, the questions archaeology could ask were becoming more pointed. The stakes were higher, the answers more complex yet increasingly within reach. A new generation of archaeologists set aside the once colorful tales of adventure and got down to a different kind of business.

ONE OF THESE ARCHAEOLOGISTS was Dorothy Garrod. She tackled archaeology the way a physicist might break down the structure of a proton; she was thorough and methodical and had an eye fastened to detail. Her good friend, Gertrude Caton-Thompson (1888–1985), another notable early woman archaeologist, referred to a "Garrod tradition of eminence in the advancement of scientific learning."[2] Garrod came from brainy stock—a family of important scientists. Though a woman, she matched precedent and eventually won recognition as a "towering figure" in archaeological history, one who exerted an "enormous intellectual legacy."[3] Her lasting influence in the field was as deep as the sites she dug. Standing on the edge of an excavation unit in the Paleolithic cave site of Tabun in Palestine, Garrod gazed down at a cleared span of nearly 600,000 years of human history, a layer cake of history made of old hearth ash, tools, bones, and crumbled red ocher, all cascading beneath her boots in varying shades of soil.

Her quest was prehistory—human origins and the first seeds of agriculture, to be specific—and she considered the revolutionary new discoveries of early man (yes, women too) throughout Europe and beyond to be "the very life-blood of our science." She seized the opportunities available in new dating methods (radiocarbon), constructed new and reliable chronologies, led complicated field excavations, found some of the earliest evidence for domestication of the dog, and became the first female professor at Cambridge University. She worked with leading men of the day as a highly respected colleague, if not a leader. Her training was tough—one mentor made her place her hand in a bag, feel the stone tools, and identify them by touch alone[4]—and she traveled far and wide to work in the cave sites where our ancestors once lit warm fires during a dark and cold Ice Age.

Like the women archaeologists who came before her, Garrod traveled to remote corners of the earth under harsh conditions—in some regions she couldn't go anywhere without an armed escort—yet this legendary woman remains a little opaque to the public eye. Highly reserved, she didn't showcase her personal life or write a string of gushing letters home, and until recently, very few photographs of Garrod were known to exist. So little personal information was available that for years rumors claimed she had burned everything—notebooks, pictures, letters, and sketches.

"DOROTHY WAS UNIQUE, rather like a glass of pale fine stony French white wine."[5] That was the way one colleague characterized her. Another gave a nod to her "sound judgment," explaining that Garrod was "a good mixer, with a genuine interest in people, whatever their age, status, or diversified affairs. Her retentive memory, wide reading and interest outside her own subject, such as music (she played the violin and flute), fitted her to contribute something of interest, fun, or wit to most type of conversation." *But*, "if bored or displeased she could be devastatingly silent, sultry, abrupt, or unco-operative."[6]

Yet another portrait of Garrod gives us a woman both "reserved, assured, delightful" in the field, and "frightened, ill at ease" in hierarchical situations or when giving public lectures.[7] Evidently, she was tricky to read and sensitive to circumstance.

An obituary written for her noted that "partly through natural reticence, partly through social conventions of earlier life, she seldom alluded in general conversation, professional circles apart, to her own work and position, or to the international community of distinguished scientists in which, by inheritance and personal achievement she moved so easily." She was quiet, modest, some said shy. By the list of her extensive publications, she was busy too.

Garrod was born on May 5, 1892. Her grandfather was knighted Sir Alfred Garrod. He was a professor at King's College Hospital and was later endowed with the fancy title of Physician Extraordinary to Queen Victoria. He had three sons, two of whom became outstanding scientists and the third a poet. Garrod had a zoologist uncle, and her father, Sir Archibald Edward Garrod, was famous for pioneering a new field of medicine dealing with metabolic troubles. He was Regius Professor of Medicine at Oxford, a Fellow of the Royal Society, and honorary member of countless medical institutions, clubs, and organizations at home and abroad. The Garrod household kindled the scientific spirit, which, in the words of Dorothy Garrod's famous father, acts as a check as well as a stimulus, a spirit "restraining too eager flights of the imagination and too hasty conclusions."[8] This spirit of restraint deeply influenced Garrod's approach to archaeology.

By the grace of so many clever minds in the family, the Garrods enjoyed social prestige and upper class wealth and comfort. Although little information exists about Garrod's mother, Laura Elizabeth Smith, it is known that she had a scientific upbringing also. Her father was a surgeon famed for the dexterity of his hands. That attribute was passed onto Garrod, holding her in good stead when she would one day gently lift fragile human bones out of clingy clay-rich earth.

Vignettes of Garrod's childhood are scare. She studied with a governess and received a sound drumming in math, history, and Latin.[9] She went to a boarding school and entered Cambridge as an undergraduate in 1913, though, like all women at the time, she was not recognized as a full student and could not receive a degree.

One of the most formative aspects of Garrod's early life was tragedy: the unexpected loss of *three* brothers, one at a time. All were star-bound in their respective careers, promising futures almost guaranteed, but Alfred (already a doctor) was killed in France while serving for the Army Medical Corps; Thomas died of wounds while serving in France as well; and Basil, the youngest, died in a flu pandemic on the eve of his demobilization. World War I ripped through the lives of the Garrod family, and the heartbreak was not confined to just kin. It is rumored that the man Garrod was to marry died too, "swept away"[10] by war's terror. A piercing grief left Garrod alone as an only child, bereft of her lover, and staring down a life where her chosen career—still undetermined—would now fill massive amounts of empty space. She told a friend during that dark time that she had resolved "to try and compensate her parents, as far as lay in her power, by achieving a life they could feel worthy of the family tradition."[11] No wonder her writing was devoid of self. She was stiff with loss, determined to prove her own worth as the equal not just to a man but rather to three.

LIKE SOLDIERS RETURNING home from war, Garrod was shell-shocked. The trauma of losing her brothers led her to join her parents in Malta, an island nation off the coast of Italy, where her father was engaged in medical work. To help ease his daughter's distracted mind, Sir Archibald suggested that she tour the scenic ruins of Stone Age agriculturalists and all the other successors who built their temples and roads there. Garrod wandered alone, mulling over what she might do with the rest of her life. At the time, she was considering architecture.[12] Yet something in the history she was surrounded by pushed her toward archaeology. When she returned home she enrolled in Oxford's anthropology program. From there, a quick sequence of events catapulted her into the field where she belonged.

University connections introduced her to L'Abbé Henri Breuil. A priest-cum-prehistoric archaeologist with a great interest in cave paintings, the Abbé Breuil became a formative teacher in Garrod's life. Working in the ancient caverns by an acetylene lamp, exploring "impossible caves in a Roman collar and bathing dress,"[13] he would decipher the shapes of galloping horses and bison from a mess of scribbled lines. Whenever a new deco-rated cave was found, the Abbé Breuil was called in first. He believed that the masterful depictions of animals (think Lascaux, the first page in almost any art history textbook), rendered in ocher shades of red and yellow, outlined in blacks, highlighted in chalky whites, and all mixed with lustrous animal fat, symbol-ized magic rituals for hunting. Many of his theories about why cave paintings were made have not stood the test of time, and his interpretations have been questioned, but during his heyday he was the authority in Paleolithic archaeology. Under his tutelage, Garrod was taken to see the ancient caves of Niaux and others. They crawled on their bellies to get through tight, slippery cave tunnels and squeezed through crevices to find "all sorts of wonders; bison modelled in clay, and portraits of sorcerers, and footprints of Magdalenian man."[14]

In the galleries of these pitch-black caves, paintings esti-mated to be as old as eighteen thousand years were illuminated by candlelight. Animals sketched in charcoal danced in flickering light. Garrod's excitement about Paleolithic archaeology, very deep history, and human origins was similarly ignited. She would be a prehistorian. One of Garrod's good friends stated in an inter-view that "the determination to be a prehistorian and particularly in the Stone Age, came over her in one second, like a conver-sion. She was, after the War, in turmoil, what was she to do with her life? And, it came over her in a flash, that was what she was to do."[15] Her direction now sure, she became the Abbé Breuil's full-time pupil in 1922. They would remain friends and respected colleagues for the next forty years.

The Abbé Breuil was a teacher who didn't bother to lecture; on the contrary, he waited until smart questions were asked and then he answered them at length. Garrod absorbed knowledge through dialogue. If she couldn't conjure up an intelligent question, there was silence. Like the Abbé Breuil, Garrod was a Roman Catholic, and their conversations included subject matter both scholarly and spiritual. Garrod had converted to the church at the time of her brothers' deaths during World War I. Both archaeologists were confronted with a history—an evolutionary history of vast time—that did not jibe with their shared religious beliefs. Did they wrestle with this conflict as they worked together excavating the cave floors? Did they try to reconcile the bones they unearthed with the biblical account of creation they believed in?

As the evidence continued to suggest a very ancient world, one that extended far beyond the estimated age of the planet that the Church espoused (4000 BC), Garrod struggled with the issue. She even withdrew from her work until she could make peace with her intellectual and spiritual quandary.[16] Resolution was found through the influence of French philosopher and Jesuit priest Pierre Teilhard de Chardin, who abandoned the Book of Genesis for a looser interpretation of change over time. He aligned that change with the cosmos and his notion of ever progressing "centeredness." Whatever the details of his now obscure philosophy, it was a balm to Garrod, and she felt comfortable from that point on to dig into the question of who we are and where we came from. It was likely one of the first debates between creationist and evolutionist points of view.

LEFT: A variety of early stone tools
RIGHT: Ancient stone tomb and assorted religious relics

At the Abbé Breuil's persuasion, Garrod took on a gigantic research project. She pulled together all the loose strands of information—the scattered site reports, artifacts stored in different museums, and partial field notes from numerous Paleolithic excavations throughout Britain—and made sense of them all by organizing the disparate bits of information, resolving discrepancies, and folding the whole package into a large, clear picture of early human development, published as *The Upper Paleolithic in Britain*. Still considered a classic, the work helped align understandings of human evolution in Britain with what was already recorded in mainland Europe, a long-time goal of archaeologists who had longed to make connections between the two places. For her effort, Garrod was awarded a Bachelor of Science degree from Oxford in 1924, and the road to some high-profile digs was paved.

From the start, Garrod's intellectual quest was to throw light on the Upper Paleolithic as a whole.[17] At the turn of the century, the question of human origins was cutting-edge stuff. Take into account the fact that in previous centuries artifacts found in a freshly plowed farmer's field were believed to be supernatural, celestial, or organic. Stone tools were thought to be the by-product of thunder; ancient pottery was believed to grow naturally in the earth, bowls taking rounded shape in soft soil, narrow jugs in the walls of rodent holes.[18] There were times when no distinction could be made between fossilized seashells, sparkling crystals, and ivory carved with decorations by a human hand; they were just strange pretty things come from above. Angel craft. Solidified stardust. Now, it was these very stone tools that Dorothy was so expert in identifying. She could pick up a chert flake, date it by style alone, set it within a chronology, and draw conclusions about our human ancestry tool by tool.

Her breakthrough moment came at the site of Devil's Tower in Gibraltar. The Abbé Breuil had advised her to look at the site, and it proved to be a career maker. The Rock of Gibraltar is a giant mass of limestone bursting up through the sea off the coast of Spain. Human bones were picked up on site as early as 1770, and for years following, a few teeth would appear now and then, a femur, a jawbone, and eventually some more bones of a "very primitive type" seeming to belong to that "period before the age of 'polished stone.'"[19] In 1917, the Abbé Breuil had spotted some more bones tucked into a small cave at the foot of a steep vertical rock peak. Garrod arrived several years later and stayed to excavate for a total of seven months. It was during this time that she made the monumental discovery of a Neanderthal child, and pieced it together from well-preserved broken skull fragments. In the mid-1920s, the impact of this discovery was explosive. Here was new evidence for the growing tree of evolution. Sealing the deal for Garrod's career, she matched her huge find with a perfect report—perfectly readable to other professionals, though almost impossibly dry and technical for the layperson. "Few documents of comparable importance" wrote a friend of Garrod "have been more tersely and coolly written by a beginner who has just added a chapter to history."[20] Her careful excavations and meticulous analysis of every soil layer, bird bone, tool type, and worn tooth were intensely thorough and put her in good stead with the scientific community.

In 1997 a scholar named Pamela Jane Smith found a lost archive in the Musée des Antiquités nationales outside Paris. The rumors about the burned papers were false. In it was a lifetime of Garrod's handwritten field notes, photo albums, and site documents. One photograph in particular gives a telling glimpse of Garrod's work and her love for it. She named the remains of the Neanderthal child, assessed to be male, about five years old, Abel. The picture shows a thirty-four-year old Dorothy smiling, sitting above the excavation trenches, cupping the small skull in her hands. She looks really happy. In her personal album this photo was given pride of place, decorated on each corner by a little red star.[21]

While Jane Dieulafoy had Susa and Harriet Boyd Hawes had Gournia, Garrod's fieldwork extended all over the map. Because she was tracing human origins, she moved through the Old World as our ancestors might have: full of curiosity and with deliberation. During her career, field explorations took her to Palestine, Kurdistan, Anatolia, Bulgaria, France, Spain, and Lebanon. With the exception of one excavation at a French site called Glouzel that left a bitter taste in her mouth (the site was a hoax, salted with fake artifacts and highly publicized to embarrassing degree), all of her sites were major. The Abbé Breuil provides a good summary of the string of her accomplishments that drew attention to Ms. Garrod's capacity for more distant undertakings, and was the means of her being appointed to the direction of researches in caves of the Near East, to which, in 1928 onwards, she gave all her time. "With various collaborators she explored in 1928 the cave of Shukba (27 kilometers north of Jerusalem), and those of Zarzi and Hazar Merd in Southern Kurdistan. After that she explored the group of caves and rock-shelters of the Wady el-Mughara near Haifa... These last excavations were particularly lucky, admirably conducted and excellently described."[22]

Garrod's work in the caves of the Wady el-Mughara at Mount Carmel—where she was the director of joint excavations undertaken there by the British School of Archaeology in Jerusalem and the American School of Prehistoric Research—lasted from 1929 to 1934 and produced some of the most important human fossils ever found—more Neanderthals and a rare, nearly complete female burial.

> Garrod was responsible for designing the excavation strategies for several, sometimes simultaneous, excavation sites during seven seasons, soliciting and budgeting finances, setting up camps, choosing, hiring, training and supervising her co-workers, arranging for equipment and supplies, dealing with British Mandate officials, and maintaining cordial relationships with the local Arab employees and their community. She was notified of all finds and made the decisions on how to preserve and to catalogue the abundant archaeological remains. The analysis of artifacts required an extraordinary effort... Garrod was responsible for analysis of all this material, writing field reports and publication of results. She handled these formidable tasks expertly.[23]

ABOVE: Dorothy Garrod and two of her field colleagues

The archaeological remains from the Wady el-Mughara included an astonishing 87,000 stone tools alone. Garrod undertook all of the classifying and cataloging of these artifacts by herself.[24] It was a task that could have lasted a less able person a lifetime.

The results of her work eventually produced a detailed chronological understanding of the Stone Age in the Levant region, published in *The Stone Age of Mount Carmel* (1937). The book was a triumph, and Garrod was awarded honorary doctorates from the University of Pennsylvania, Boston College, and Oxford University. Thanks to her, the Levant had become the best understood area of human evolution in the world at the time, unmatched in its clarity of sequence. Garrod was not just a woman making advances in science but an archaeologist taking giant strides through the field, and her influence was legendary. By 1939, she was considered one of Britain's finest archaeologists.

WHEN WORKING IN the field, Garrod was regularly in the company of male colleagues, students, and assistants who were all smart and commendable professionals. But more often than not, her field crews were composed exclusively of *women*. Whether it was by chance (the best qualified people all happened to be female) or outright preference (to advance a feminist agenda), it was no longer the "boys' club" that reigned unquestioned. There was now a sort of recognized ladies' club in the fields of archaeology, all of whom were conducting groundbreaking research.

The "ladies' club" had existed as only a fleeting entity until Garrod formalized it. Its spirit harks back to a vignette that Margaret Murray, an archaeological predecessor of Garrod who taught hieroglyphics and excavated in Egypt in 1902, wrote while delighting in feminine companionship on a site. There had

ABOVE: Garrod and her all-female excavation team at the Mount Carmel Caves, 1929

been a suspicious noise in the camp one night, a sign that some looters might be causing trouble. Murray suggested they have a look:

> "Oh, yes, go if you like." But Mr. Stannus was shocked at the idea of three defenceless women 'going into danger' without a man to protect them, so he gallantly came too. He got the shock of his life when we three women joined hands and danced with a great variety of fancy steps all the way from the camp to the dig. The joining of our hands was precautionary, for fancy steps on those tumbled sand-heaps in the uncertain light of the moon is a tricky business. Poor Mr. Stannus, he had always been accustomed to the Victorian man's ideal of what a lady should be, a delicate fragile being who would scream at the sight of a mouse.[25]

The little moonlit dance in which three women linked arms to buck the conventional view of ladylike meekness foreshadowed a larger movement. Garrod's decision to create a work force almost entirely of women was unusual for her day, and it certainly commanded attention from the establishment. She hired local Arab women to assist on her excavations, since they worked extremely well and the money she paid them went directly to the needs of their families.[26] During her first season at Mount Carmel her excavation team was nearly all female: the Arab girls did the basic digging, and four university-educated women—Elinor Ewbank, Mary Kitson, Harriet Allyn, and Martha Hackett—assisted her. The really heavy physical work was taken on by local men.[27] Garrod's actions gave field feminism a push, and as one of her crew, a woman named Yusra, explained: "We were extremely feminist you see because all the executive and interesting part of the dig was done by women and all the menial part ... by men." [28] The tables had turned.

Whether or not Garrod and her women colleagues ever danced by moonlight is their secret, but they definitely enjoyed a ritual glass of sherry. "Sabbath" sherry was at 6:00 PM sharp, and even the "mud, muck, ooze upon the floor, torn tents and thunder—all were forgotten as the sherry bottle was opened." [29] Archaeological field conditions remained as challenging as ever, and the women were exposed to heat, murderous humidity, dirty drinking water, storms, and disease. Some became quite ill. But sherry was a cheering curative, a reason to toast the hardships of the field—so rough in the moment, so good when told as stories later on.

Garrod's camaraderie with other pioneering women archaeologists (though she was normally regarded as "the boss") extended throughout her career. Her most enduring relationships—both as professionals and as close friends—were with two women: Germaine Henri-Martin, the daughter of an archaeologist whose site Garrod had worked on in her post-graduate days, and Suzanne de St. Mathurin. All three excavated together at different sites; all were prehistorians. Many of the excavations they conducted were in France, and as their achievements were increasingly recognized in the press and within academic circles, the French affectionately nickname them *Les Trois Grâces* (The Three Graces). The three pioneers remained together even in death—their archives at the Musée des Antiquités nationales are kept together. Each woman left the others her favorite photos and keepsakes. And so they remain bound.

Les Trois Grâces joined together late in their careers to aid a significant site in peril, a cave called Ras el-Kelb in Lebanon. The year was 1959, and two tunnels were being blasted through the rock; the integrity of the Paleolithic cave would be destroyed. Damage had already been done to the site years before when a railway had been laid down adjacent to it, and now the Director of Antiquities in Lebanon had requested that Garrod come out immediately and conduct a rescue dig. *Les Trois Grâces* arrived on the scene.

What they encountered was a new and fairly unprecedented ingredient in the field of archaeology: modern development. Construction projects pose a serious threat to archaeological sites—a blast of dynamite here or grading bulldozer there can erase evidence of thousands of years of human history in a moment's time. Whereas once the biggest hurdle to accessing an archaeological site was distance (permissions were also tricky), now the graver concern was how much *time* do we have before the site is gone? Today, the rescue of sites slated for destruction is called salvage archaeology. Archaeologists excavate what they can and do their best to understand the cities and structures of yesterday before tomorrow's skyscrapers and highways take their place.

For Garrod and her two collaborators, in addition to sandstorms and lice; there were now ear-splitting drills, construction dust, and relentless hammers banging metal all day. The women worked for seven weeks straight in an environment of deafening jackhammers. Wet tents and snakes would have been preferable. Some of the site's strata, or the soil layers, were also as hard as cement. No shovel stood a chance. Garrod decided that the only way to truly assess what the prehistoric site contained was to cut out blocks of the cement-like earth called breccia with high-power drills and send them to the National Museum in Beirut for analysis. At least it would be quiet there.

DOROTHY GARROD IS a little like a calmer and more introverted Gertrude Bell. The ferocity of their intellect and the intensity, the sheer volume of their life's achievements unites them. Both women had lost men important to them and subsequently threw themselves unconditionally into their work. Both had exceptionally close relationships to their fathers. Bell was the first woman to take a First in history at Oxford, thereby changing the academic terrain for other women and proving that ideas about a woman's supposed intellectual inferiority were nonsense, and Garrod ratcheted the ladder even higher. In 1939 she became Disney (nothing to do with Walt) Professor of Archaeology at the University of Cambridge. It was an electrifying event, and female students at all English universities were overjoyed by the news.

Her application for the position at Cambridge began, "I beg to submit myself as a candidate." She didn't think she would get it. There were very few women in teaching positions at the university in 1939, and Dorothy's application was in competition with those of a large number of accomplished male scholars. Full membership for women in the university system still had not been granted, and archaeology—especially prehistory—was seen as manly territory. Women might make headway in literature and poetry, but in the field?

It was precisely Garrod's unmatched excellence in the field that brought her victory. No other applicant had her credentials for original site discoveries. Many of her competitors were "armchair archaeologists" whose greatest contributions to archaeology were born from library books and pipe smoke. When she was elected professor, women scholars and students throughout Europe were elated. The Garrod tradition of scientific achievement continued, and a woman now held one of the most respected and esteemed positions in science. Although she shied away from all the publicity that descended upon her (actually devoured her), Garrod had done what she set out to do. She had proven herself the worth of a man, of even three men, and of all the male archaeologists who had come before her and who worked beside her. Right after the announcement of her professorship, Garrod confided to her friend Gertrude, "I wish my father had been alive, and the others." Her father had died recently. The men in her life—father, brothers, fiancé—must have cheered from on high. Courage and perseverance had brought her to her goal.

Here she is at age fifty, a portrait that captures the newly appointed professor's physical presence:

> Although 50 years old, her upright, well-knit figure, moving quietly and unselfconsciously, gave an impression of controlled energy of mind and body... She appeared taller than her 5 ft. 2 in., with noticeably small, delicate, but strong hands which seldom fumbled. Her steady eyes were dark brown and when greeting people flickered momentarily; the lids seemed to curtsey. Her thick crisply waving dark hair was worn short. The pleasant quiet voice, pitched rather low, had a tendency to drop at the end of a sentence. Her movements were unhurried but not slow, and even under pressure she imparted an air of repose. This paradox of tranquility combined with a life of sustained energy, was a characteristic rarely met with to such a degree.[30]

Garrod had worked through the complications of field life and had always loved teaching small groups and classes, yet within the ivory tower she hit her biggest challenge yet. Simply becoming one of the first women professors did not eradicate centuries of discrimination. From out of the wide-open field and into the windowless meeting rooms of Cambridge, she felt stifled and clipped. Her associates proved to be cagey and self-aggrandizing. The faculty committees and boards were mired in hierarchy and personality conflicts. Her task as Disney Professor was to help reorganize the archaeology department and enhance its studies in prehistory. Although she enjoyed this aspect of her work, the rigmarole of university life and policy sucked her dry. Even her lectures suffered. Naturally reserved, she delivered lectures that were notoriously tedious and dull. One student complained of presentations with "never a light or bright moment."[31] University life was oppressive to Garrod. She stayed on as faculty until 1954, continuing her fieldwork and research when possible, but at age sixty she retired, happily, and like some bird that had once been caged, she bolted, wings spread, toward her "years of fulfillment" back in the field.

She began work on the coasts of Lebanon and Syria, which contained earthy ribbons of evidence showing late Pleistocene sea levels, and began a search for ancient shorelines. In determining the contours of the former Ice Age sea, she could locate inland sites that had once been coastal. These were the ideal spots where a person would want to make camp: caves with ocean views (and good fishing) surrounded by land where plants could be gathered and animals caught. Garrod also had a new tool up her sleeve. With the advent of radiocarbon dating, she could obtain certain dates for some of the artifacts she uncovered. Her chronologies of the Paleolithic period in Palestine and Lebanon grew more robust, more comprehensive, more invaluable to archaeological understandings of how humans became human.

ABOVE: Garrod, always devoted to conducting excellent fieldwork

THE SOCIETY OF Antiquaries of London was founded in 1707, and its Royal Charter (the same today as it was then) is to enable "the encouragement, advancement and furtherance of the study and knowledge of the antiquities and history of this and other countries." For its first two hundred years of operation, women were denied any role in the society. Even those who had advanced archaeological knowledge in England and abroad were ignored. In 1968 that pattern was reversed when the society awarded Dorothy Garrod its grand Gold Medal. She was seventy-six years old. In her acceptance speech Garrod made a point of mentioning the historical absence of women within the society; she issued a soft reprimand. She also proclaimed to the society fellows a new truth—one directed specifically at the society but applicable to the entire field of archaeology. She summarized the unstoppable arrival of women to a field once denied them by remarking that, at last, here was "the long-awaited and by some, long-dreaded day, when the gates of the citadel were finally opened to the Amazons."[32]

Garrod had secured entry into the field of archaeology to a degree no woman before her had. As she tore down those gates, a rush of other women followed. Some ran alongside her. It was in the post–World War I climate that several women gained a stronger foothold in the sciences they loved. Garrod just happened to be, perhaps, the most outstanding and certainly one of the most trenchant figures.

Why Garrod chose archaeology as her life's passion is a question that harks back to her younger days when she lost her three brothers, and perhaps her future husband, and thereon decided to make her life a worthy thing. To decide on a scientific field was almost a foregone conclusion, but archaeology veered significantly from medicine or zoology. Could Garrod have found some attraction in selecting the "ultra-masculine" scientific field *least* accessible to her, one that required her to forsake the daily comforts of a clean desk and clothes for work more physically rigorous and demanding? She may have felt that archaeology offered her more room to prove something, to venture into territory where history was not just the subject studied but something she could harness herself, change the direction of. By breaking into the field as a woman, she could *make* history.

Garrod's passion for prehistory and human origins also ties into broader themes about why archaeology is such a persistent love, a source of captivation, even today. People never lose interest in learning about lost treasures or hearing a good piece of evidence concerning our peculiarly smart species: making the first fire, writing with reeds, burying kings with enough soldiers and wealth to survive the afterlife.

In a world (a Western world) where creation stories are scoffed at as fanciful, where science has replaced magic, and where spirituality has been given a run for its money by individualism and consumerism, archaeology is the rare endeavor that emphasizes objectivity but also calls for emotion and touches excitable hearts. People don't like things sugar-coated as much as they do science-coated, and archaeology offers up the greatest stories about human origins, intrigue, and drama with a nice big pinch of truth. These are the facts, the archaeologists assure us. Garrod's attraction to archaeology was probably much like people's today: here was a way to dig up some great stories to share, methodically, carefully, and have a rather fun time doing it.

EPILOGUE

. . . . .

EXCAVATIONS

*C*amels, deserts, archaeology, solitude, and women's lives lived fearlessly: a romantic combination that appeals to us folk bound to laptops, an apartment lease or mortgage, and routine. The pioneering women archaeologists experienced a brand of adventure that evokes dreamy wanderlust and longing for the time when a woman could gallop across deserts on a horse wearing impractical but fetching clothes, a knife strapped to her leg beneath her petticoat, a bag full of ammunition and letters, no return ticket, tea and conversation in tents. These women seemed so free in a way we no. longer are, tethered as we are to email and cell phones and appointment books. Nor can we truly escape from our own Western culture, as Coke cans, fast food, and neon lights greet us upon arrival in most corners of the world. In the late nineteenth and early twentieth century, to go away was really and truly to be gone.

After exploring the lives of each of the seven women in this book, I realized that except for Dorothy Garrod, none of them were young women when they embarked on their archaeological travels, only to return to the equivalent of settled suburban life after a fleeting moment in a faraway place. Nor did they build enviable careers by age thirty. On the contrary, their professional and personal achievements were a slow burn.

While most of the ladies chronicled here had at least an interest in archaeology and history when they were young, archaeology often sneaked into their lives in unexpected ways and at unexpected times. Amelia Edwards found her passion for Egyptology by chance on the Nile. She was thirty years old when she set out looking for life's new path, though. Advancing archaeological work in Egypt was not something she had in mind. To do so, she compromised a lucrative career as a novelist to start learning hieroglyphics in her late thirties, mastered it, and became a middle-aged Egyptologist.

Zelia Nuttall had loved Mexican archaeology since reading picture books made of ancient symbols and codes as a child before bedtime, but she did not venture out into the archaeological field itself until age *fifty-three*. Accustomed to life in a big fancy house with servants and distinguished guests to entertain, she was downright excited about camping in an abandoned quarantine station for weeks on a deserted island so she could dig. You never do know when life's best adventure will present itself.

Jane Dieulafoy's career in archaeology was handmaiden to her marriage. Had she married a different man, Susa might never have been their shared dream. Still actively excavating in Morocco just before she succumbed to fever at age sixty-five, Dieulafoy followed her passion for archaeology all the way to death's door, and her taste for rigorous fieldwork only deepened as she aged. She and Marcel excavated and went on arduous journeys their whole lives. It was a rare form of sustainable adventure.

Gertrude Bell was forty-four years old when she started flirting with the (married) man she loved. She was forty-five when she rode solo on a "desperate and heroic" journey through Syrian deserts.[1] She never packed her first bags looking for archaeology per se, but it later became a passion and a search that defined and shaped the route of her journeys. It was on the eve of her fiftieth birthday that she bought her first house in Baghdad and finally settled into a career she liked (and one immensely suited to her). Looked at a certain way, Bell's life, for all its epic accomplishments, was a vagabond's existence. She was the girl who figures out what she wants only after trying everything else first.

Harriet Boyd Hawes's career path resembles a trajectory more common to today than a hundred years ago. She attended college and then graduate school, achieved success as a field archaeologist with her work at Gournia, and at age thirty-four married and started a family. Although this last step seems normal by contemporary standards, back then her delay to wed and breed was the exception. After the babies were born, she left them behind for a spell when called back to nurse on the frontlines of war—another unusual decision for that time.

Then there is Agatha Christie, who claimed that her life didn't really begin until age forty. It was after she and her first husband had divorced and she was en route to the site of Ur, via the Orient Express, that she saw a major transition not just in occupation but in geography, as she and second husband Max spent much of their time living on Middle Eastern sites. For Christie, archaeology was a late-life encounter. She never saw it coming, and when it suddenly appeared before her, she embraced it (and Max) fully, sticking with the field for another thirty years.

Dorothy Garrod's relationship with archaeology did start when she was a young woman, a student crawling through the painted caves with the Abbé Breuil. Yet at age *sixty,* just when most professors would be considering a comfortable retirement, Garrod was back out in the field with more fire than ever, excavating on the coasts of Lebanon and Syria. She had started a whole new, post-Cambridge, chapter in her life.

Although there is nothing surprising about women accomplishing great things as they mature, it is refreshing to discover women who were not only ground-breaking scientists but also unafraid and willing to change course midstream. In our youth-obsessed culture, it is wonderful to see that life really can begin at forty, and that one's best and most satisfying adventures may be yet to come.

What is it, then, about archaeology that inspired these women to make it their life's work, to decide it was that chance worth taking? Does the field attract a certain type of personality? T.S. Eliot once called archaeology the "reassuring science." It was the endeavor that made Gertrude Bell feel "most well," the mystery Agatha Christie was hooked by, the "beloved science" that Zelia Nuttall felt moved to advance. Its allure is timeless. The power of archaeology lies in its rare alchemy: the blend of history, discovery, travel, and adventure. What lies buried underfoot is its own kind of frontier: secrets of the past remain as mysterious to us as the moon.

Archaeology is an engagement with questions about what makes us human, what events and which tools brought us here today, how our ancestors saw the world, and what we can learn not just about the past but also from it. Passions run high for hidden history. They always have. Its study reveals not just the foundations and story blocks of humanness but also all of the strange, amazing, and unbelievable things our species has done, like rip beating hearts from each other's chests, build thousands of life-size clay soldiers to protect a dead emperor, paint gorgeous creatures on cave walls, figure out how to cultivate plants to farm, and worship a universe full of complex deities through art and objects and little effigies made of bone, stone, and metal. We've built golden shrines and constructed temples and churches that take our breath away with their beauty. Humans have created innumerable mysteries for other humans to unravel.

Each mystery offers up potential for new understandings of who we are, of what happened and why. Did this civilization topple that one? Why do some cultures and even some species, like the Neanderthal, disappear? Which trade networks were in place, and how exactly did turquoise stones move through the southwestern United States and out to the shores of the Pacific? Why? As any archaeologist might wonder with a scratch of the head, gazing out at a partially excavated site where the walls and

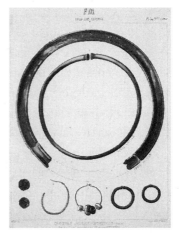

LEFT: Decorated pottery and antler bone
RIGHT: Metal necklace fragments, bead earrings, and pendants

the artifacts and footprints of ancient houses haven't yet made full sense—what does it all mean? Archaeology is that incredible job where you get to ask huge questions. And, for each answer you find, a dozen new questions open up. It's juicy work.

Archaeology is also the very beautiful process of excavation and artifact analysis: the artisan's process of rinsing dirt from clay beads, blowing gritty sand from gold, reconstructing the broken pieces of a finely painted porcelain pot. The material culture is innately poetic. The tools for excavation are seductive in their own right: a favorite steel trowel, rumpled leather gloves, compass, Agatha Christie's cold cream and knitting needle.

For these Victorian-era women attracted to the field, archaeology was a means to escape the humdrum of society life, where women passed their days focused on home and hearth and were viewed as feeble little things in need of a man to watch over them. A time when feminine weakness was desirable, pale skin and fainting spells were kind of sexy. By extreme contrast, archaeology was worldly—outdoorsy. It was a line of work that kept one healthy in both body and spirit, suntanned and muscular. The first women archaeologists were drawn to a new science that afforded them the opportunity for intense intellectual stimulation—to entertain some of the questions described above—but also as a means to cleverly buck the establishment.

I don't believe any of the ladies chose archaeology because it would prove a woman's worth; none of them were steadfast champions of women's rights, though some may have been feminists. Their reasons for going into the field were their own. Edwards had wanderlust. Jane Dieulafoy loved Marcel. Nuttall wanted to work in Mexico and cared deeply for indigenous culture and history. Bell was passionate for ruins and desert drama. Boyd Hawes wanted to study in Greece, while Christie was feeling brave and found the unexpected. Garrod had a family reputation to live up to. These were their private love affairs.

They were also dedicated to science, not social change. Nevertheless, as a result of their actions, academic circles, professional organizations, and even newspapers were acknowledging that female scientists were reaching new milestones. Women could endure the hardships of camping, digging, traveling; they could mastermind surveys, excavations, and field crews; they could gather the evidence together, publish, and contribute meaningfully to a science that had long denied them the chance to speak. By their own accord and strength, they kicked down shut doors. The Victorian stereotype of a weak woman was overturned. The first women archaeologists gave the women's rights movement ammunition to demonstrate equality between the sexes.

Perhaps a certain type of personality is attracted to archaeology—an adventurous one to be sure. A little headstrong. Passionate and willing to take some risks. For just as people surely discouraged the seven women whose stories are told here, for every new undergraduate majoring in archaeology today, someone will ask, "But is there a career in that? Any money? Are you sure?" Archaeology has never been work for the faint of heart. It takes some daring. Its reward is the process (never the treasure alone): the experience of excavation and the little things you find along the way.

As Bell said, it simply feels good to do archaeology. As an archaeologist myself who has worked on digs in the Middle East and Europe and across North America, I can say that there is a delicious feeling in abandoning ordinary codes of dress and behavior and basic expectations like looking nice, being fashionable, feeling pretty. It can be delightful to work a pickaxe until you've got biceps like tough little lemons and hair so dirty it stays in a bun *sans* clip. Archaeology is a bit like camping with a sense of great underlying purpose and productivity; we are gathered here to uncover the past. Imagine what it was like in Victorian days to shrug off corsets and high-neck dresses. To ditch tea parties for the open road.

The story of archaeology's pioneering women captures a critical moment in time when a group of women challenged the mode of thinking that confined them. They embody a burst of daring and freedom, as much as they do the birth of a new science. Beginning with Amelia Edwards's sentimental prose about the ruins of Egypt and ending in Dorothy Garrod's concise scientific explanations and chronologies of human evolution, the seven women here represent the arc of archaeology's own history: from romantic to pragmatic, from story to science.

Their legacy also stikes personal chords, even today. Something in the way they'd kick their donkeys to a trot, dig deeper in the saddle, board the creaky dinghy with gusto, carry a rifle, and swing the pickaxe until their strength wore out. The first women archaeologists remind us that the world is full of opportunity for the brave. They remind us that the world is big—big and wonderful.

GLOSSARY

CHRONOLOGY: A sequence, and some would say a science, of arranging time. When archaeologists establish a "chronology" it means that they have put historical events into order and assigned approximate dates to certain styles of pottery, tools, etc.

CODEX: Precursor to the modern-day book. The word "codex" usually refers to European manuscripts with pages all bound on one side. Codices that survive from pre-Conquest Mexico, however, are like picture books set on screenfolds. They open up like an accordion. These ancient Mexican codices contain images that are "read" as a sequence. Stretched out, they resemble ornate murals.

DAHABEEYAH: Means the "golden boat" in Arabic. These houseboats were very popular in Egypt's Victorian heyday. An Englishman by the name of Thomas Cook championed the vessels as the premier way for Western tourists to experience the sites of the Nile. Upper-class Egyptians also liked the luxurious form of transportation. In 1869, the steamship was introduced to the Nile and dahabeeyahs fell out of use.

DIG: More than a verb. A "dig" is shorthand for a full-blown archaeological excavation. Will you be going on a dig this summer? You bet.

DIRT: Actually *not* the same as soil. Dirt is something you wash off, the muck that makes one dirty. It can be a little loose soil under the fingernails, or plain dust, grime, and technically even poop.

FIELD: Hardly a meadow or agricultural plot. The "field" is where people venture to conduct their "fieldwork." This means that they are out of the library, away from a desk, and are conducting original, hands-on research of some kind often with a trowel in hand.

KNICKERS: British underwear. Commonly used in the expression, "Well now, don't go getting your knickers in a twist!" In Victorian days, knickers were typically *open crotch pants* that fell to just below the knee and were trimmed with ribbons, buttons, and lace.

MULETEER: One who handles the moody, kicking beasts of burden essential for packing equipment in and out of an archaeological site.

OBJECTIVE: As in "to be objective." Implies that all thinking has been done without the influence of emotion and/or personal bias. To be objective is, in theory, to base any decision or conclusion on facts alone.

POTSHERD: A broken piece of a pot. Potsherds are ubiquitous on many archaeological sites, and just because they are broken, that doesn't mean they aren't valuable! Sherds are collected, analyzed, sometimes glued back together, and used to help assess how old a site is and who occupied it.

RADIOCARBON: A radioactive isotope of carbon (also known as carbon-14). Its existence was confirmed in the mid-1950s and it allows archaeologists to date any object that was once a living thing (e.g., bones or wood) up to 60,000 years old. The testing process is complicated, but suffice it to say it works, and it revolutionized archaeology. It allowed archaeologists to pursue new "absolute" dating methods versus "relative" ones.

SEASON (archaeological): The limited period of time in which a crew of archaeologists descend upon a site with pickaxes, shovels, and spades. A season—typically a summer, though in very hot climates a winter—is often referenced as a discrete period of time; e.g., Season I was highly productive! Season II revealed a new addition to the site. Season III was a disaster and bad weather ruined everything. There is usually one "season" per year.

SOIL: Earth—the rich mixture of organic compounds and debris that buries an archaeology site and holds it close.

STRATIGRAPHY: The natural and cultural layers of an archaeological site. Each "stratum" contains soil and artifacts related to each other. The overall stratigraphy of a site is what allows an archaeologist to say, "We have strata representing the Bronze Age, the Iron Age, and up through the Hellenistic (Greek) period." Yippee!

SUBJECTIVE: All of us are subjective creatures. We see the world through our own lens of personal experience, beliefs, culture, feelings, and instincts. Subjectivity is an emotional response to life, its events, and the artifacts left behind. A subjective interpretation of the archaeological record relies on gut instinct and is colored by personal experience.

TELL: A large mound, normally found in the Middle East, containing the remains of numerous settlements and/or civilizations all stacked up on top of each other. A tell looks like a very strange hill.

THEORY: An idea of what happened, a possible explanation, a well-educated guess. Some people keep theories as "pets" (pet theories are ideas that get a lot of special attention). Archaeologists will craft a theory about what a certain site tells us about the past. Field excavations and site comparisons will prove that theory true or false. Here is a sample theory: North America was first populated by people who crossed the Bering Strait land bridge 15,000 years ago. True or false?

ZIGGURAT: Like a terraced pyramid with a flat top, a temple or shrine. Often considered to be the dwelling places of gods, ziggurats are found in Iran and the Mesopotamian Valley; the earliest are approximately 6,000 years old.

NOTES

·　·　·　·　·

INTRODUCTION: FIELD NOTES

1　Mary Ann Levine, "Presenting the Past: A Review of Research
 on Women in Archaeology," *Archaeological Papers of the American
 Anthropological Association* (1994), 24.

2　In 1870, Queen Victoria expressed her view on women's rights as
 follows in a private letter to Sir Theodore Martin: "I am most anxious
 to enlist everyone who can speak or write to join in checking this mad,
 wicked folly of 'Women's Rights', with all its attendant horrors, on
 which her poor feeble sex is bent, forgetting every sense of womanly
 feelings and propriety. Feminists ought to get a good whipping. Were
 woman to 'unsex' themselves by claiming equality with men, they
 would become the most hateful, heathen and disgusting of beings and
 would surely perish without male protection."

3　Jean-Jacques Rousseau, as cited in an excerpt by Albertine-Adrienne
 Necker de Saussure (1844), in *Victorian Women: A Documentary Account
 of Women's Lives in Nineteenth-Century England, France, and the United
 States*, eds. Erna Olafson Hellersten, Leslie Parker Hume, and Karen M.
 Offen (Stanford, CA: Stanford University, 1981), 62.

4　William Acton, M.R.C.S., *The Functions and Disorders of the
 Reproductive Organs*, 8th American ed. (Philadelphia, 1894), 208–212.

5　August Deboy, *Hygiène et physiologie du mariage*, 153 ed. (Paris, 1880),
 17–18, 92, 94–95, 105–109.

6　Elizabeth Missing Sewell, *Principles of Education, Drawn from Nature
 and Revelation, and Applied to Female Education in the Upper Classes*
 (New York, 1866), 396–397, 450–451.

7　Quote from Gertrude Bell, in a letter home dated 1892.

8   Amelia Edwards, *A Thousand Miles Up the Nile:*
    A woman's journey among the treasures of ancient Egypt
    (Coventry, UK: Trotamundas Press Ltd., 2008), 13.

CHAPTER I: AMELIA EDWARDS

1   Amelia Edwards, *A Thousand Miles Up the Nile:*
    A woman's journey among the treasures of ancient Egypt
    (Coventry, UK: Trotamundas Press Ltd., 2008), 128–129.

2   Ibid, 19.

3   Ibid, 140.

4   Digital copy of *A Thousand Miles Up the Nile.*
    Available at www.touregypt.net/amelia/chapter18.html

5   Brenda Moon, *More Usefully Employed:*
    Amelia B. Edwards, Writer, Traveller and Campaigner for Ancient Egypt
    (London: Egypt Exploration Society, 2006), 10.

6   Ibid, 11.

7   Ibid, 7.

8   Ibid, 1.

9   Ibid, 14.

10 Edwards, *A Thousand Miles Up the Nile*, 293.

11 Joan Rees, *Writings on the Nile: Harriet Martineau,*
    Florence Nightingale, Amelia Edwards (London: Rubicon, 1995).

12 Edwards, *A Thousand Miles Up the Nile*, 225.

13 Ibid, 18.

14 Ibid, 240.

15 Ibid, 31.

16 Ibid, 294.

17 Ibid, 191.

18 Ibid, 122.

19 Ibid, 30.

20 Ibid, 85.

21 Today the site of Abu Simbel has been relocated. In the 1960s,
    the temple was raised, transported, and rebuilt to protect it from the
    flooding of Lake Nasser.

22 Julia Keay, *With Passport and Parasol: The Adventures of Seven Victorian*
    Ladies (London: BBC Books, 1989).

23 Digital copy of original 1891 edition of *A Thousand Miles Up the Nile*. Available at http://digital.library.upenn.edu/women/edwards/nile/nile.html.

24 Ibid.

25 Ibid.

26 Excerpt from a letter written by Amelia Edwards to Edward Abbot in 1881, as cited in Brenda Moon, *More Usefully Employed*, 153–154.

27 Today, it's known as the Egypt Exploration Society.

28 Moon, *More Usefully Employed*, 203.

29 Ibid, 224.

30 Barbara S. Lesko, "Amelia Blanford Edwards, 1831–1892," www.brown.edu/Research/Breaking_Ground/bios/Edwards_Amelia%20Blanford.pdf

CHAPTER 2: JANE DIEULAFOY

1 Eve Gran-Aymerich, "Jane Dieulafoy, 1851–1916," *Breaking Ground: Pioneering Women Archaeologists* (Ann Arbor, MI: University of Michigan Press, 2004), 56.

2 *New York Times* obituary for Madame Dieulafoy, May 28, 1916.

3 Gran-Aymerich, "Jane Dieulafoy, 1851–1916," 60.

4 Ibid, 36.

5 Ibid.

6 Jane Dieulafoy, "The Excavations at Susa," *Harper's Monthly Magazine* 75, no. 445 (June 1887), 1.

7 "Uses Hubby's Wardrobe," *New York Morning Journal*, excerpted in Margot Irvine, "Jane Dieulafoy's Gender Transgressive Behaviour and Conformist Writing," in *Gender and Identities in France*, eds. Brigitte Rollet and Emily Salines (Portsmouth, UK: University of Portsmouth, School of Languages and Area Studies, 1999).

8 Dieulafoy, "The Excavations at Susa," *Harper's Monthly Magazine*, 7.

9 Gran-Aymerich, "Jane Dieulafoy, 1851–1916," 42.

10 Dieulafoy, "The Excavations at Susa," *Harper's Monthly Magazine*, 6.

11 Ibid, 4.

12 Ibid, 10.

13 Gran-Aymerich, "Jane Dieulafoy, 1851–1916," 46.

14 Dieulafoy, "The Excavations at Susa," *Harper's Monthly Magazine*, 10.

15 Ibid.

16 Ibid, 12.

17 Ibid, 17.

18 Ibid, 18.

19 Ibid.

20 Ibid.

21 Gran-Aymerich, "Jane Dieulafoy, 1851–1916," 50.

22 Ibid, 51.

23 Photo in the archives of the Department of Oriental Antiquities at the Louvre Museum, Paris.

24 Irvine, "Jane Dieulafoy's Gender Transgressive Behaviour and Conformist Writing." Translation courtesy of Catherine Stevenson and Margaret Dubin, 14.

25 *New York Times* obituary for Madame Dieulafoy dated May 28, 1916.

26 Irvine, "Jane Dieulafoy's Gender Transgressive Behaviour and Conformist Writing." Translation courtesy of Catherine Stevenson and Margaret Dubin, 17.

27 Ibid.

28 Ibid.

29 Gran-Aymerich, "Jane Dieulafoy, 1851–1916," 67.

30 Professor Margot Irvine, personal communication, November 2009.

31 Gran-Aymerich, "Jane Dieulafoy, 1851–1916," 59.

32 Ibid, 63.

33 Irvine, "Jane Dieulafoy's Gender Transgressive Behaviour and Conformist Writing," 15.

34 She could also be a mother. According to the 1916 *New York Times* obituary for Dieulafoy, "Mme. Dieulafoy was the mother of a son and daughter." Oddly enough, this fact is not mentioned in other sources. Perhaps Dieulafoy kept motherhood quiet (or relied intensely on wet nurses and nannies) so as to keep her career unhindered.

CHAPTER 3: ZELIA NUTTALL

1 D.H. Lawrence, *The Plumed Serpent* (Ware, Hertfordshire, UK: Wordsworth Editions Ltd., 1995), 25.

2 Ibid, 32.

3 Ibid, 33.

4   Ibid, 25.

5   Nancy O. Lurie, "Women in Early Anthropology," *Pioneers of American Anthropology*, ed. June Helm (Seattle: University of Washington Press, 1966), 29–83. Italics are author's own.

6   Alfred M. Tozzer, "Zelia Nuttall, Obituary." *American Anthropologist* 35 (1933): 475–482.

7   The crystal skull now resides in the Musée du quai Branly; the other was proven to be a fake.

8   Letter on file at the Bancroft Library, University of California, Berkeley.

9   Today, the museum houses a collection of 3.8 million objects.

10   Ross Parmenter, "Glimpses of a Friendship: Zelia Nuttall and Franz Boas. (Based on their Correspondence in the Library of the American Philosophical Society of Philadelphia)," in *Pioneers of American Anthropology,* ed. June Helm (Seattle: University of Washington Press, 1966), 88.

11   "The World's Columbian Exposition: Idea, Experience, Aftermath," http://xroads.virginia.edu/~ma96/WCE/title.html.

12   Parmenter, "Glimpses of a Friendship," 88–91.

13   It was eventually examined, very much so. Native American burial sites were excavated in high volume with little concern given to the living descendants of those whose graves were being unearthed.

14   A letter from Zelia to Boas dated 1909, cited in Ross Parmenter article detailed above.

15   And still does. Nobel Prize–winning author Octavio Paz later lived there. Today the house is a cutting-edge center for new music technology called Fonoteca Nacional.

16   Tozzer, "Zelia Nuttall, Obituary," 475–482; also in "Zelia Nuttall," *Women Anthropologists: A Biographical Dictionary,* eds., Ute Gacs, Aisha Khan, Ruth Weinberg, and Jerrie McIntyre (Chicago: University of Illinois Press, 1989), 269–274.

17   Lawrence, *The Plumed Serpent,* 24.

18   Tozzer, "Zelia Nuttall, Obituary," 475–482.

19   Lurie, "Women in Early Anthropology," 29–83.

20   Zelia Nuttall, ed., *The Codex Nuttall: A Picture Manuscript From Ancient Mexico* (New York: Dover Publications, Inc., 1975). Introduction by Arthur G. Miller.

21 Zelia Nuttall's "New Light on Drake: a collection of documents relating to his voyage of circumnavigation 1577–1580," Hakluyt Society series 2, no. 34, 1914.

22 Ibid.

23 Zelia Nuttall, "The Island of Sacrificios," *American Anthropologist*, New Series 12, no. 2 (1910), 257.

24 Ibid, 273.

25 Ibid, 257–258.

26 Ibid.

27 Ibid, 267.

28 Parmenter, "Glimpses of a Friendship," 125.

29 Nuttall, "The Island of Sacrificios," 280.

30 Ibid.

31 Tozzer, "Zelia Nuttall, Obituary," 475–482.

32 "Zelia Nuttall," *Women Anthropologists*, 272.

33 Zelia Nuttall, "The New Year of the Tropical Indigenes: The New Year Festival of the Ancient Inhabitants of Tropical America and its Revival" Bulletin, *The Pan American Union*, 1928, 62, Washington, 71.

34 Ibid, 73.

CHAPTER 4: GERTRUDE BELL

1 As cited in Dorothy Van Ess Book Review of *Gertrude Bell: From Her Personal Papers, 1914–1926* by Elizabeth Burgoyne in *Middle East Journal* 16, no. 1 (1962), 93.

2 *The Letters of Gertrude Bell: selected and edited by Lady Bell, D.B.E.* Vol. 1 (New York: Boni and Liveright, 1927). Also available online at: http://gutenberg.net.au/ebooks04/0400341h.html

3 Unless otherwise noted, all Gertrude Bell letter excerpts quoted throughout the chapter are from the digital archives of The Gertrude Bell Project, Newcastle University in Tyne, www.gerty.ncl.ac.uk/letters.php.

4 Gertrude Bell, *The Desert and the Sown* (London: W. Heinemann, 1907).

5 Ibid, 198.

6 *The Letters of Gertrude Bell: selected and edited by Lady Bell*, online.

7   The Gertrude Bell Project, online.

8   Georgina Howell, *Gertrude Bell: Queen of the Desert, Shaper of Nations* (New York: Farrar, Straus and Giroux, 2007), 37.

9   *The Letters of Gertrude Bell: selected and edited by Lady Bell,* online.

10   Ibid.

11   Ibid.

12   Julia M. Asher-Greve, "Gertrude L. Bell, 1868–1926," in *Breaking Ground: Pioneering Women Archaeologists* (Ann Arbor: University of Michigan Press, 2004), 142–197.

13   *The Letters of Gertrude Bell: Selected and Edited by Lady Bell,* online.

14   In Memoriam notice of Bell, written by Colonel E. L. Strutt, editor of the *Alpine Journal*, November 1926.

15   The Gertrude Bell Project, online.

16   Bell, *The Desert and the Sown*, 12.

17   The Gertrude Bell Project, online.

18   Ibid.

19   Ibid.

20   Asher-Greve, "Gertrude L. Bell, 1868–1926," 168.

21   Vita Sackville-West, *Passenger to Tehran* (New York: George H. Doran, 1927), 57–62.

22   The Gertrude Bell Project, www.gerty.ncl.ac.uk/.

23   Ibid.

24   That protection was tragically compromised when looting of the museum began in April 2003 during the U.S. invasion of Iraq; over 15,000 objects were taken. To date, approximately half of those have been reclaimed.

25   Max Mallowan, *Mallowan's Memoirs* (London: Collins, 1977), 42.

26   The Gertrude Bell Project, online.

27   Ibid.

28   Bell's finest biographer, Georgina Howell, depicts a rare moment of intimacy between Bell and Doughty-Wylie. It took place in Bell's bedroom: "Her happiness was an intoxication ... He pressed her to him, full of affection, and they lay down. Folded in his arms Gertrude told him that she was a virgin. His warmth and attentiveness were boundless, but when he kissed her and moved closer, put his hands on her, she

stiffened, panicked whispered 'No.' He stopped at once, assuring her that it didn't matter, and when tears came into her eyes he comforted her for a few minutes and told her nothing had changed. The he slipped away out the door." The next day Bell received a "let's be friends" letter from Dick. Georgina Howell, *Gertrude Bell: Queen of the Desert, Shaper of Nations*, 137.

29 A letter to Horace Marshall dated June 18, 1892, written by Bell from Gulahek (now Kulhek), a village situated approximately 60 miles outside of Teheran.

30 Bell, *The Desert and the Sown*.

31 Georgina Howell, *Gertrude Bell: Queen of the Desert, Shaper of Nations* provides excellent detail of the event.

32 Ibid, 417.

CHAPTER 5: HARRIET BOYD HAWES

1 Mary Allsebrook, *Born to Rebel: The Life of Harriet Boyd Hawes* (Oxford: Oxbow Books, 1992), 186.

2 Ibid, 215.

3 Vasso Fotou and Ann Brown, "Harriet Boyd Hawes, 1871–1945" in *Breaking Ground: Pioneering Women Archaeologists* (Ann Arbor: University of Michigan Press, 2004), 200.

4 Allsebrook, *Born to Rebel*, 4.

5 Ibid, 14.

6 Ibid, chapters VI and VII.

7 Ibid, 15–16.

8 Letter dated April 28, 1900, on file at Smith College archives.

9 Boyd Hawes's own reference to the Homeric quote made in her Annual Report. Homer, *Odyssey*, XIX, Butchers and Lang's Translation (London: MacMillan, 1879), 172.

10 Fotou and Brown, "Harriet Boyd Hawes, 1871–1945."

11 Ibid, 214.

12 Ibid.

13 Cheryl Claassen, ed., *Women in Archaeology* (Philadelphia: University of Pennsylvania Press, 1994), 45.

14 Harriet Boyd, "Excavations at Gournia, Crete" *Annual Report of the Board of Regents of the Smithsonian Institution Showing the Operations, Expenditures and Condition of the Institution for the Year Ending June 30, 1904* (Washington: Government Printing Office, 1905), 562; also in Fotou and Brown, "Harriet Boyd Hawes, 1871–1945," 217.

15 Allsebrook, *Born to Rebel*, 99.

16 Harriet Boyd, "Excavations at Gournia, Crete," *Annual Report, 1904*, 563.

17 Allsebrook, *Born to Rebel*, 102.

18 Harriet Boyd, "Excavations at Gournia, Crete," *Annual Report, 1904*, 563.

19 The young archaeologist Edith Hall, another Smith graduate, assisted Boyd Hawes on site. She later created her own successful career as an archaeologist.

20 Allsebrook, *Born to Rebel*, 10

21 Boyd, "Excavations at Gournia, Crete," *Annual Report, 1904*.

22 Allyson McCreery, "Digging for Equality: Women in Archaeology in the Victorian Era" (Unpublished Honors History Thesis, Temple University, Philadelphia, 2007).

23 Fotou and Brown, "Harriet Boyd Hawes, 1871–1945," 224.

24 Allsebrook, *Born to Rebel*, 230.

25 Ibid, 230.

26 Ibid, 131.

27 U.S. Bureau of the Census (2003), www.census.gov/population/socdemo/hh-fam/tabMS-2.pdf.

28 Allsebrook, *Born to Rebel*, 228.

29 Ibid, 228.

30 *The New York Times*, February 26, 1901, as cited in *Born to Rebel*, 135.

31 Fotou and Brown, "Harriet Boyd Hawes, 1871–1945," 235.

CHAPTER 6: AGATHA CHRISTIE

1 Agatha Christie, *Agatha Christie: An Autobiography* (Glasgow: William Collins Sons & Co. Ltd, 1977), 372.

2 Ibid.

3   Ibid, 9.

4   Ibid, 11.

5   Ibid, 14.

6   Ibid, 95.

7   Ibid, 134.

8   Ibid.

9   Ibid, 172–175.

10 Ibid, 274.

11 Janet Morgan, *Agatha Christie: A Biography*
    (New York: HarperCollins, 1986), 81.

12 Ibid, 115.

13 Christie, *An Autobiography*, 357.

14 Ibid, 362.

15 Ibid, 389.

16 Morgan, *Agatha Christie*, 179.

17 Christie, *An Autobiography*, 406.

18 Ibid, 410.

19 Morgan, *Agatha Christie*, 185.

20 Agatha Christie, *Come, Tell Me How You Live*
    (New York: Simon & Schuster, Inc., 1946), 50.

21 Ibid, 85–88.

22 Charlotte Trümpler, ed., *Agatha Christie and Archaeology*,
    (London: The British Museum Press, 2001), 189.

23 Christie. *An Autobiography*, 472.

24 Ibid, 483.

25 Christie, *Come, Tell Me How You Live*, 57.

26 Trümpler, *Agatha Christie and Archaeology*, 229.

27 Ibid, 233; also Christie, *Come, Tell Me How You Live*, 117.

28 Christie, *Come, Tell Me How You Live*, 119.

29 Trümpler, *Agatha Christie and Archaeology*, 45.

30 Ibid, 45–47.

31 Agatha Christie, *Death on the Nile*
    (New York: Bantam Books, 1972), 204.

32 Morgan, *Agatha Christie*, 208.

CHAPTER 7: DOROTHY GARROD

1 Dorothy Garrod, et al., "Excavation of a Mousterian Rock-shelter at Devil's Tower, Gibraltar," *Journal of the Royal Anthropological Institute* 58 (1928): 91–113.

2 Gertrude Caton-Thompson, "Dorothy Annie Elizabeth Garrod, 1892–1968 (obituary)," *Proceedings of the British Academy* 65 (1969), 339–361, 340.

3 Geoffrey A. Clark, book review in *Bulletin of the American Schools of Oriental Research*, no. 326, (2002), 81–83.

4 Lorraine Copeland, "Dorothy Garrod's excavations in the Lebanon" in *Dorothy Garrod and the Progress of the Palaeolithic: Studies in the Prehistoric Archaeology of the Near East and Europe*, eds. William Davies and Ruth Charles (Oxford: Oxbow Books, 1999), 164.

5 Bruce Howe, personal correspondence to Ofer Bar-Yosef, Jane Callander, and Smith, 1998. As cited in Pamela Jane Smith, "From 'small, dark and alive' to 'cripplingly shy': Dorothy Garrod as the first woman Professor at Cambridge," (Cambridge, UK: Lucy Cavendish College, Cambridge University), n.d.

6 Caton-Thompson, "Dorothy Annie Elizabeth Garrod, 1892–1968"

7 Smith, "From 'small, dark and alive' to 'cripplingly shy.'"

8 Quote taken from "The Scientific Spirit in Medicine: Inaugural Sessional Address to the Abernethian Society," *St. Bartholomew's Hospital Journal*, 20, 19, 1912.

9 Ofer Bar-Yosef and Jane Callander, "Dorothy Annie Elizabeth Garrod, 1892–1968" in *Breaking Ground: Pioneering Women Archaeologists* (Ann Arbor: University of Michigan Press, 2004), 381.

10 Ibid, 382.

11 Caton-Thompson, "Dorothy Annie Elizabeth Garrod, 1892–1968" 341.

12 Ibid, 342.

13 Smith, "From 'small, dark and alive' to 'cripplingly shy."

14 From a letter Dorothy Garrod wrote to her cousin in 1921, as cited in Ibid.

15 Pamela Jane Smith, *A Splendid Idiosyncrasy: Prehistory at Cambridge 1915–50* (Oxford: British Archaeological Reports, 2009), 72.

16 Caton-Thompson, "Dorothy Annie Elizabeth Garrod, 1892–1968" 343.

17 Dorothy's application for Professorship in *Dorothy Garrod and the Progress of the Palaeolithic: Studies in the Prehistoric Archaeology of the Near East and Europe* (Oxford: Oxbow Books, 1999), 16.

18 Bruce G. Trigger, *A History of Archaeological Thought*, (Cambridge: Cambridge University Press, 1989), 47.

19 Dorothy Garrod et al., "Excavation of a Mousterian Rock-shelter at Devil's Tower, Gibraltar," *Journal of the Royal Anthropological Institute*.

20 Caton-Thompson, "Dorothy Annie Elizabeth Garrod, 1892–1968" 344.

21 Pamela Jane Smith et al., "Dorothy Garrod in words and pictures," *Antiquity* 71 (1997): 265.

22 Abbé Breuil's letter of recommendation, as cited in *Dorothy Garrod and the Progress of the Palaeolithic*, 17.

23 Smith, "From 'small, dark and alive' to 'cripplingly shy.'"

24 Dorothy's application for Professorship, *Dorothy Garrod and the Progress of the Palaeolithic*, 16.

25 Margaret Alice Murray, *My First Hundred Years*, (London: W. Kimber, 1963), 116.

26 William Davies, "Dorothy Garrod—A Short Biography" in *Dorothy Garrod and the Progress of the Palaeolithic: Studies in the Prehistoric Archaeology of the Near East and Europe*. (Oxford: Oxbow Books, 1999), 6.

27 Brian Boyd, "Dorothy Garrod and the Natufian Culture," in Ibid, 213.

28 Smith, "From 'small, dark and alive' to 'cripplingly shy.'"

29 Ibid.

30 Caton-Thompson, "Dorothy Annie Elizabeth Garrod, 1892–1968" 339.

31 Smith, "From 'small, dark and alive' to 'cripplingly shy.'"

32 Bar-Yosef and Callander, "Dorothy Annie Elizabeth Garrod, 1892–1968," 413.

CONCLUSION: EXCAVATIONS

1 Rosemary O'Brien, ed., *Gertrude Bell: The Arabian Diaries, 1913–1914* (Syracuse, NY: Syracuse University Press, 2000).

BIBLIOGRAPHY

. . . . .

Allsebrook, M. *Born to Rebel: The Life of Harriet Boyd Hawes*. Oxford: Oxbow Books, 1992.

Becker, M. J., and P. P. Betancourt. *Richard Berry Seager: Pioneer Archaeologist and Proper Gentleman*. Philadelphia: University of Pennsylvania Museum Publication, 1997.

Bell, Gertrude Lowthian. *Persian Pictures: A Book of Travel*. London: R. Bentley and Son, 1894.

——. *The Desert and the Sown*. London: W. Heinemann, 1907.

——. "The Vaulting System of Ukheidar." *The Journal of Hellenic Studies* 30 (1910): 69–81.

——. "The East Bank of the Euphrates from Tel Ahmar to Hit." *The Geographical Journal* 36, no. 5 (1910): 513–537.

——. *Amurath to Amurath*. London: W. Heinemann, 1911.

——. *Gertrude Bell: the Arabian diaries, 1913–1914*. Edited by Rosemary O'Brien. Syracuse, NY: Syracuse University Press, 2000.

——. A Journey in Northern Arabia. *The Geographical Journal* 44, no. 1 (1914): 76–77.

——. *Palace and Mosque at Ukhaidir: A Study in Early Mohammadan Architecture*. Oxford: Clarendon Press, 1914.

——. *The Letters of Gertrude Bell, selected and edited by Lady Bell*. New York: Boni and Liveright, 1927.

——. *The Earlier Letters of Gertrude Bell*. London: E. Benn, 1937.

——.*The Arab War: Confidential Information for General Headquarters*. London: The Golden Cockerel Press, 1940.

——. *Teachings of Hafiz*, translated from the Persian by Gertrude Bell. London: Octagon Press for the Sufi Trust, 1979.

————. *The Churches and Monasteries of the Tur'Abdin.*
London: Pindar Press, 1982.

Bell, Gertrude, Arthur Evans, and Henry Trotter. "The Balkan Peninsula: Discussion." *The Geographical Journal* 41, no. 4 (1913): 336–340.

Boyd, Harriet A. "Gournia—Report of the American Exploration Society's Excavations at Gournia, Crete, 1901–1903." In *Transactions of the Department of Archaeology Free Museum of Science and Art, vols. 1 and 2.* Philadelphia: University of Pennsylvania Department of Archaeology, 1904.

————. "Excavations at Gournia, Crete." *Annual Report of the Board of Regents of the Smithsonian Institution Showing the Operations, Expenditures and Condition of the Institution for the Year Ending June 30, 1904.* Washington: Government Printing Office, 1905.

Caton-Thompson, Gertrude. "Dorothy Annie Elizabeth Garrod, 1892–1968 (obituary)." *Proceedings of the British Academy* 65 (1969): 339–361.

Cohen, G. M., and M. S. Joukowsky, eds. *Breaking Ground: Pioneering Women Archaeologists.* Ann Arbor: University of Michigan Press, 2004.

Christie, Agatha. *Come, Tell Me How You Live.*
New York: Simon & Schuster, Inc., 1946.

————. *Death on the Nile.* New York: Bantam Books, 1972.

————. *Agatha Christie: An Autobiography.*
Glasgow: William Collins Sons & Co. Ltd, 1977.

Claassen, Cheryl, ed. *Women in Archaeology.*
Philadelphia: University of Pennsylvania Press, 1994.

Davidson, Robyn. *Tracks: A Woman's Solo Trek Across 1,700 Miles of Australian Outback.* New York: Vintage Books, 1980.

Davies, William, and Ruth Charles, eds. *Dorothy Garrod and the Progress of the Paleolithic: Studies in the Prehistoric Archaeology of the Near East and Europe.* Oxford: Oxbow Books, 1999.

Diaz-Andreu, Margarita, and Marie Louise Stig Sørensen.
Excavating Women: A history of women in European archaeology.
London and New York: Routledge, 1998.

Dieulafoy, Jane. "The Excavations at Susa." *Harper's Monthly Magazine* 75, no. 445 (June 1887).

———. *La Perse, la Chaldée et la Susiane: relation de voyage.*
Paris: Hachette, 1887.

———. *À Suse; journal des fouilles 1884–1886, par Mme Jane Dieulafoy.*
Paris: Hachette, 1888.

———. "Le théâtre dans l'intimité." "Naïs, La Sulamite, Farce nouvelle du pâté et de la tarte." "Farce nouvelle très bonne et fort joyeuse du cuvier, Défiance et malice." Conférences de M. Philippe Berger, M. Bernardin, [et] M. Émile Picot. Paris: P. Ollendorff.

———. *Isabelle la Grande, reine de Castille, 1451–1504.*
Paris: Hachette, 1920.

———. *À Suse.* Tehran: Mu'assasah-'i Ch p va Intish r t-i D nishg h-i Tihr n, 1977.

———. *Perse, la Chaldée et la Susiane.* Tehran: Kit bfur sh -i Khayy m, 1982 (or 1983).

———. *En mission chez les Immortels: journal des fouilles de Suse, 1884–1886.*
Paris: Phebus, 1990.

Du Cros, Hilary, and Laurajane Smith, eds.
Women in Archaeology: A Feminist Critique. Canberra: The Australian National University, 1993.

Edwards, Amelia. *A Thousand Miles Up the Nile: A woman's journey among the treasures of ancient Egypt.* Coventry, UK: Trotamundas Press Ltd., 2008 (first copyright 1878).

Eliot, T.S. "Tradition and the Individual Talent," in *The Norton Anthology of Theory and Criticism.* New York: W.W. Norton, 2001.

Emberley, Julia. "Gertrude Lowthian Bell in Mesopotamia," in *Writing, Travel and Empire: In the Margins of Anthropology.* Edited by Peter Holme and Russell McDougall. London: I.B. Tauris & Co. Ltd., 2007.

Engelbach, Reginald. *Riqqeh and Memphis VI,* with chapters by M.A. Murray, H. Flinders Petrie, and W.M. Flinders Petrie. London: British School of Archaeology in Egypt, 1915.

Fagan, Brian. *From Stonehenge to Samarkand: An Anthology of Archaeological Travel Writing.* Oxford: Oxford University Press, 2006.

Field, Henry. *North Arabian Desert Archaeological Survey, 1925–50,* with contributions by Evert Andrau, Dorothy Garrod, and Eric Schroeder. Cambridge, MA: Peabody Museum, 1960.

Flanders, Judith. *Inside the Victorian Home: A Portrait of Domestic Life in Victorian England.* New York: W.W. Norton, 2003.

Gacs, Ute, Aisha Khan, Ruth Weinberg, and Jerrie McIntyre. *Women Anthropologists: A Biographical Dictionary,* Zelia Nuttall: Chicago: University of Illinois Press, 1989: 269–274.

Garrod, Dorothy Anne Elizabeth. *The Upper Paleolithic Age in Britain.* Oxford: The Clarendon Press, 1926.

——. "Note on Three Objects of Mesolithic Age from a Cave in Palestine." *Man* 30 (1930): 77–78.

——. "The Palaeolithic of Southern Kurdistan: Excavations in the Caves of Zarzi and Hazar Merd." *Bulletin of American School of Prehistoric Research* 6 (1930): 13–43.

——. "Mesolithic Burials from Caves in Palestine." *Man* 31 (1931): 145–146.

——. *A new Mesolithic industry: the Natufian of Palestine.* London: Royal Anthropological Institute of Great Britain and Ireland, 1932.

——. *A New Species of Fossil Man.* London: Illustrated London News and Sketch, Ltd., 1932.

——. "The Stone Age of Palestine." *Antiquity* 8 (1934): 146.

——. "The Upper Palaeolithic in the light of recent discovery." *Proceedings of the Prehistoric Society* 4 (1938): 1–26.

——. "The Cave of Lascaux Near Montignac, Dordogne." *Man* 43 (1943): 42.

——. Environment, tools & man; an inaugural lecture. Cambridge, England: Cambridge University Press, 1946.

——. "A Transitional Industry from the Base of the Upper Paleolithic in Palestine and Syria." *The Journal of the Royal Anthropological Institute of Great Britain and Ireland* 81, nos. 1, 2 (1951): 121–130.

——. "The Middle Palaeolithic of the Near East and the Problem of Mount Carmel Man." *The Journal of the Royal Anthropological Institute of Great Britain and Ireland* 92, no. 2 (1962): 232–259.

——. "Primitive man in Egypt, Western Asia and Europe," in *Palaeolithic Times,* by Dorothy A.E. Garrod and in *Mesolithic Times,* by J.G.D. Clark. Vol. 1, chapter 3. Cambridge, England: Cambridge University Press, 1965.

———. "Transition From Mousterian to Perigordian: Skeletal and
   Industrial [and Comments and Replies]." *Current Anthropology* 7,
   no. 1 (1966): 33–50.
———. "More on the Fate of the 'Classic' Neanderthals."
   Current Anthropology 7, no. 2 (1966): 204–214.
Garrod, Dorothy. *The Transition from Lower to Middle Palaeolithic and
   the origin of modern man : international symposium to commemorate
   the 50th anniversary of excavations in the Mount Carmel Caves*. Edited
   by Avraham Ronen. Oxford: Bureau of Archaeological Research
   International Series 151, 1980.
Garrod, D.A.E., L.H.D. Buxton, G. Elliot Smith, and D.M.A. Bate.
   "Excavation of a Mousterian Rock-shelter at Devil's Tower, Gibraltar."
   Journal of the Royal Anthropological Institute 58 (1928): 91–113.
Garrod, D.A.E., and D.M.A. Bate, eds.
   *The Stone Age of Mount Carmel: Excavations at the Wady el-Mughara
   Vol. 1*. Oxford: Clarendon Press, 1937.
Garrod, D.A.E., B. Howe, and J.H. Gaul. "Excavations in the cave of
   Bacho Kiro, North-East Bulgaria." *Bulletin of the American School of
   Prehistoric Research* 15 (1939): 46–126.
———. "The stone age of Mount Carmel: report of the Joint Expedition
   of the British School of Archaeology," in *Report of the Joint Expedition
   of the British School of Archaeology in Jerusalem and the American School
   of Prehistoric Research, 1929–1934*. New York: AMS Press, 1980.
Gesell, G.C. "History of American Excavations on Crete."
   In Crete Beyond the Palaces: Proceedings of the Crete 2000 Conferences.
   Philadelphia: INSTAP Academic Press, 2004.
Gill, Gillian. *Agatha Christie: the woman and her mysteries.*
   New York: Free Press, 1990.
Hamilton, Sue, Ruth D. Whitehouse, and Katherin I. Wright, eds.
   Archaeology and Women: Ancient and Modern Issues.
   Walnut Creek, CA: Left Coast Press, Inc. 2007.
Hawes, Harriet Boyd. "Review: The Discoveries in Crete by
   R.M. Burrows." *The Classical Journal* 4, no. 2 (1908): 89–91.
———. "Review: Excavations in the Island of Mochlos by Richard B. Seager."
   Classical Philology 7, no. 3 (1912): 366–369.

———. "A Gift of Themistocles: The 'Ludovisi Throne' and the Boston Relief." *American Journal of Archaeology* 26, no. 3 (1922): 278–306.

———. "Review: Fouilles Exécutés Mallia: Premier Rappor 1922–1924 by Fernand Chapouthier; Jean Charbonneaux." *American Journal of Archaeology* 34, no. 1 (1930): 107–109.

———. "Memoirs of a Pioneer Excavator in Crete." *Archaeology* 18, no. 2 (1965): 94–101.

———. "Memoirs of a Pioneer Excavator in Crete Part II." *Archaeology* 18, no. 4 (1965): 268–276.

Hawes, Charles Henry, and Harriet Boyd Hawes. *Crete: The Forerunner of Greece*. London: Harper & Bros, 1909.

Hawes, Harriet Boyd, Blanche E. Williams, Richard B. Seager, and Edith H. Hall. *Gournia, Vasiliki, and Other Prehistoric Sites on the Isthmus of Ierapetra, Crete, excavations of the Wells-Houston-Cramp expeditions, 1901, 1903, 1904*. Philadelphia: American Exploration Society, 1908.

Hellersten, Erna Olafson, Leslie Parker Hume, and Karen M. Offen, eds. *Victorian Women: A Documentary Account of Women's Lives in Nineteenth-Century England, France, and the United States*. Prepared under the auspices of the Center for Research on Women at Stanford University. Stanford, CA: Stanford University Press, 1981.

Hill, Stephen. *Gertrude Bell (1868–1926): A selection from the photographic archive of an archaeologist and traveller*. Newcastle, UK: Department of Archaeology, The University of Newcastle Upon Tyne, 1977.

Howell, Georgina. *Gertrude Bell: Queen of the Desert, Shaper of Nations*. New York: Farrar, Straus and Giroux, 2007.

Huxley, D. *Cretan Quests: British Explorers, Excavators, and Historians*. London: British School at Athens, 2000.

Irvine, Margot. "Jane Dieulafoy's *Gender Transgressive Behaviour and Conformist Writing*." In *Gender and Identities in France: Working Papers on contemporary France Vol. 4*. Edited by Brigitte Rollet and Emily Salines. Portsmouth, UK: University of Portsmouth, School of Languages and Area Studies, 1999.

Keay, Julia. *With Passport and Parasol: The Adventures of Seven Victorian Ladies*. London: BBC Books, 1989.

LaChapelle, Dolores. *D.H. Lawrence: Future Primitive.*
  Austin, TX: University of Texas Press, 1996.
Levine, Mary Ann. "Presenting the Past: A Review of Research on
  Women in Archaeology." *Archaeological Papers of the American
  Anthropological Association,* 1994: 23–36.
Lurie, Nancy O. "Women in Early Anthropology."
  In *Pioneers of American Anthropology.* Edited by June Helm.
  Seattle: University of Washington Press 1966: 29–83.
Lawrence, D.H. *The Plumed Serpent.* Ware, Hertfordshire, UK:
  Wordsworth Editions Ltd., 1995 (originally published in 1926).
McCreery, Allyson. "Digging for Equality: Women in Archaeology
  in the Victorian Era." Unpublished Honors History Thesis,
  Temple University, Philadelphia, 2007.
Moon, Brenda. *More Usefully Employed: Amelia B. Edwards,
  Writer, Traveller and Campaigner for Ancient Egypt.*
  London: Egypt Exploration Society, 2006.
Morgan, Janet. Agatha Christie: *A Biography.*
  New York: HarperCollins, 1986.
Murray, Margaret Alice. *My First Hundred Years.*
  London: W. Kimber, 1963.
Nuttall, Zelia. "The Terra-Cotta Heads of Teotihuacan."
  American Journal of Archaeology 2 (1886):157–178, 318–330.
——. "Standard or Head Dress?" *Archaeological and ethnological papers
  of the Peabody Museum.* 1, issue 1. Cambridge Peabody Museum of
  American Archaeology and Ethnology, 1888: 1–52.
——. "Ancient Mexican Superstitions." *Journal of American Folklore* 10
  (1897): 275–81.
——. "The Fundamental Principles of Old and New World Civilizations."
  Archaeological and ethnological papers of the Peabody Museum 2.
  Cambridge Peabody Museum of American Archaeology
  and Ethnology, 1901.
——. "The Island of Sacrificios." *American Anthropologist,* New Series, 12
  no. 2 (1910): 257–295.

———. "New Light on Drake: a collection of documents relating to his voyage of circumnavigation 1577–1580," *Hakluyt Society*, series 2, no. 34 (1914).

———. "Origin of the Maya Calendar." Science 45 (1927): supplements 12 and 14.

———. "The New Year of Tropical Indigenes: The New Year Festival of the Ancient Inhabitants of Tropical America and Its Revival." *The Pan American Union*, 1928:9.

———. *The Codex Nuttall: A Picture Manuscript From Ancient Mexico.* Edited by Zelia Nuttall with an Introduction by Arthur G. Miller. New York: Dover Publications, Inc., 1975.

O'Brien, Rosemary, ed. *Gertrude Bell: The Arabian Diaries, 1913–1914.* Syracuse, NY: Syracuse University Press, 2000.

Olafson, Erna Hellerstein and Leslie Parker Hume and Karen M. Offen, eds. *Victorian Women: A Documentary Account of Women's Lives in Nineteenth-Century England, France, and the United States.* Stanford, CA: Stanford University Press, 1981.

Parmenter, Ross. "Glimpses of a Friendship: Zelia Nuttall and Franz Boas. (Based on their Correspondence in the Library of the American Philosophical Society of Philadelphia.)" In *Pioneers of American Anthropology*. Edited by June Helm. Seattle: University of Washington Press, 1966: 88–147.

Petrie, Sir William Matthew Flinders *Tombs of the courtiers and Oxyrhynkhos*, with chapters by Alan Gardiner, Hilda Petrie and M.A. Murray. London: British School of Archaeology in Egypt, 1925.

Rees, Joan. *Writings on the Nile: Harriet Martineau, Florence Nightingale, Amelia Edwards.* London: Rubicon, 1995.

Smith, Pamela Jane. *A Splendid Idiosyncrasy: Prehistory at Cambridge 1915–50.* Oxford: British Archaeological Reports, 2009.

———. "Gathering Roses in Winter." *British Archaeology* 7: 10–14.

———. "From 'small dark and alive' to cripplingly shy': Dorothy Garrod as the first woman Professor at Cambridge." Cambridge, UK: Lucy Cavendish College, Cambridge University. No pub date. Online article accessed February 2009 http://www.arch.cam.ac.uk/~pjs1011/Pams.html.

Smith, Pamela Jane, Jane Callander, Paul G. Bahn, and
    Geneviève Pinçon. "Dorothy Garrod in words and pictures."
    Antiquity 71 (1997): 265–270.
Tozzer, Alfred M. "Zelia Nuttall Obituary."
    American Anthropologist 35 (1933): 475–482.
Trigger, Bruce G. *A History of Archaeological Thought*.
    Cambridge: Cambridge University Press, 1989.
Trümpler, Charlotte, ed. *Agatha Christie and Archaeology*.
    London: The British Museum Press, 2001.
White, Nancy Marie, Lynne P. Sullivan and Rochelle A Marrinan, eds.
    *Grit-Tempered: Early Women Archaeologists in the Southeastern United
    States*. Gainesville, FL: University Press of Florida, 1999.
Wylie, Alison. "Introduction." *Archaeological Papers of the American
    Anthropological Association*, 1994: 1–4.

RECOMMENDED READING

. . . . .

Agatha Christie: An Autobiography by Agatha Christie
A History of Archaeological Thought by Bruce G. Trigger
Archaeological Papers of the American Anthropological Association Volume 5,
    Issue 1, 1994 [a valuable collection of scholarly articles examining the
    history of women in archaeology]
A Splendid Idiosyncrasy: Prehistory at Cambridge 1915–50
    by Pamela Jane Smith
*A Thousand Miles Up the Nile: A woman's journey among the treasures
    of ancient Egypt* by Amelia Edwards
Born to Rebel: The Life of Harriet Boyd Hawes by Mary Allsebrook
Breaking Ground: Pioneering Women Archaeologists.
    Editors Getzel M. Cohen and Martha Sharp Joukowsky
Come, Tell Me How You Live by Agatha Christie Mallowan
Gertrude Bell: Queen of the Desert, Shaper of Nations
    by Georgina Howell
*More Usefully Employed: Amelia B. Edwards, Writer, Traveller
    and Campaigner for Ancient Egypt* by Brenda Moon
The Desert and the Sown by Gertrude Bell
Women in Archaeology edited by Cheryl Classen

OTHER SOURCES WORTH CHECKING OUT:
The "Breaking Ground" database, a growing inventory of biographies of
    women pioneers in archaeology with continual updates and new stories
    to discover: http://www.brown.edu/Research/Breaking_Ground/
The Gertrude Bell Archive, a fascinating online search of Bell's
    photographs, letters, and diaries:
    http://gertrudebell.ncl.ac.uk/index.php

ACKNOWLEDGMENTS

*   *   *   *   *

Ladies of the Field would not have been possible without the assistance, support, and work of scholars and friends. Professor Martha Sharp Joukowsky, co-editor of the book *Breaking Ground: Pioneering Women Archaeologists,* provided early encouragement for this project; my sincere thanks for the enthusiasm and support.

Professor Margot Irvine at the University of Gelph was exceptionally helpful in my research of Jane Dieulafoy, as was Béatrice André-Salvini, Conservateur general, chef du departement des Antiquités Orientales at the Louvre, Paris. I am also indebted to Fabienne Queyroux, Conservateur en Chef at the Bibliothèque de l'Institut en Académei Français for humoring my terrible French and for helping me navigate the archive's permissions process. Catherine Stevenson and Dr. Margret Dubin are also warmly acknowledged for providing me with French translations of Jane Dieulafoy's material.

Jessica Zimmer provided me with some initial research assistance, and LeeAnn Barnes continued to be my personal "arch-angel" by forwarding me so many items of interest over the past year. Jody Michael Gordon, PhD candidate at the University of Cincinnati, Department of Classics, suggested that I consider including Agatha Christie in the book, and that suggestion was happily seized upon. Yuki Furyuya, also a PhD student at the

University of Cincinnati, Classics Department and currently working in Greece, kindly sent me a rare article written by Harriet Boyd Hawes from the Smithsonian Institute. Dr. Pamela Jane Smith is the remarkable scholar who uncovered the "lost" archives belonging to Dorothy Garrod. For her cooperation in allowing me to read and cite her work I am most grateful. Thanks must also be extended to my mother, Kathy, who joined me in Paris, saved us both with her very good French, and walked enough Metro stairs to last a lifetime. Several people read early chapter drafts: my amazing brothers Kevin and Tim Adams, and dear friends Erisa Coppernoll and Emily Cook. My husband, Matthew Hinde, read the whole manuscript (at least twice) and always brought me a steady supply of laughs and love throughout the project's duration. Thank you all.

And last, sincere thanks to my wonderful editor, Nancy Flight, whose generous insights and comments I always look forward to and value so highly. I'm also grateful to my publisher, Rob Sanders, for his ongoing vision and support. Everyone at Greystone Books is a treat to work with—special thanks also to Lara Kordic, Lara Smith, Carra Simpson, and Emiko Morita.

INDEX

. . . . .

Italicized page numbers indicate figures. Page numbers for notes are followed by "n" and the note number.

PHOTO CREDITS

* * * * *